SALE ON SALES
BUSINESS SALES

Author: Dean Sale

Copyright © 2020 Dean Sale

All rights reserved. No parts of this book may be reproduced, distributed, or transmitted in any form or by any means, electronic or mechanical, including photocopying, recording or by any information storage and retrieval system, without written permission from the author – expect for brief quotations in critical reviews, articles and other non-commercial uses permitted by copyright law.

ISBN: 978-1-8380169-0-6 (Paperback)

ISBN: 978-1-8380169-1-3 (eBook)

Dedication

To my beautiful wife Nicola, you've always believed in me.
"Tell her about it. Tell her all your crazy dreams" - Billy Joel
... I did, and we now dream together.

To my wonderful kids Ryan & Katy, I'm so proud of you both.
"Throw your dreams into space like a kite, and you do not know what it will bring back, a new life, a new friend, a new love, a new country"
- Anais Nin

To Mom & Dad, thanks for your guidance, support & love.

CONTENTS

ABOUT ME - Page 5

ABOUT THIS BOOK - Page 11

Chapter 1. WHY SALES? - Page 21

Chapter 2. SALES FUNDAMENTALS: Principals, Key Ingredients and Tips & Techniques for successful selling - Page 39

Chapter 3. WORDS, TIMING AND TONE: What you say, when you say, how you say - Page 123

Chapter 4. CLOSING: If you're not closing then you aren't selling - Page 137

Chapter 5. OBJECTION HANDLING: Use their excuses to your advantage - Page 151

Chapter 6. INFLUENCER OR DECISION MAKER? - Page 183

Chapter 7. RESEARCH AND STRATEGY: Knowledge with a plan of action - Page 191

Chapter 8. SALES ROLES: Telesales & Telemarketing, Field Sales and Account Management - Page 207

Chapter 9. EMOTIONS: Your mind and your heart - Page 227

Chapter 10. WHAT NOW? - Page 239

ABOUT ME

Hi, I'm Dean, thank you so much for buying my book.

Before we get started on this journey together, I'd like to introduce myself and let you know why I wrote this book.

Why? ...

Trust is key, you're much more likely to trust and adopt what I say within this book if you know a little more about me, what my journey has been and what I've achieved myself in sales. You're much more likely to read this book to the end too, if you're confident you'll see positive changes and results within yourself, your sales role and your bank balance.

The many people I've employed and mentored over 20 years have all started their relationships with me based on trust. I won't ask you to do anything I've not done myself and I won't ask you to do anything that I haven't asked others to do and then seen positive results produced. However, what I will ask is that you dig deep emotionally as I'm taking you back to basics with a view to resetting and moving forwards.

I want you to keep an open mind, be honest with yourself and trust me. I want you to re-evaluate your goals, push yourself more than ever and turn your wants and desires into an obsession.

As I'm building trust with you, it's important for you to know that I'm more than qualified to write this book, experienced within sales and a good example of someone that has worked hard and smart to achieve success in sales & business whilst at the same time keeping a smile on my face, a core set of values and a 'family first' attitude.

As this obviously isn't an autobiography, I'll keep this brief as I'm sure you want to get to the good stuff! Me too.

About me (in brief):

• I was 43 years old at the time of writing this book, in 2019. (Published in 2020).

• I'm married, with 2 children.

• I've been in sales for over 25 years. 18 of these years was as the co-founder and sales director of a successful telecoms company.

• I'm a kid from a council estate that has always dreamt big.

• When I was 15, I had an epiphany and my 'want' for success began. It was the first time I said, "I can, and I will".

• I flew on Concorde when I was 19 years old as a reward for sales excellence. I ran down the aisle at supersonic speed so I could feel like a superhero.

• When I was 19 years old, I set myself a goal of becoming a millionaire by the age of 45. In my early twenties I reduced this timeframe to 43.

• When I was 25 years old, I co-founded a telecoms business (with my business partner and friend) from a small office in Birmingham. We started with just £25,000 in the bank, no website, no customers and only a few employees. Over 18 years we grew to a medium sized business that employed over 40 people with a multimillion-pound turnover.

• In 2009, my business was featured in THE SUNDAY TIMES - Fast Track 100, we were ranked as the 90th fastest growing company in the UK. I collected an award at Sir Richard Branson's home.

• My business won multiple industry awards over 2 decades.

• In 2018 I sold my shares in my business. 'We created it, we built it and then we sold it' that was always our plan. I walked out of my office on my 43rd birthday! a millionaire. The goal I set when I was a teenager had been accomplished.

• Since January 2019 I've been pursuing other interests, including writing this book.

• In October 2019 I launched my new business, Sales Whizz®. Sales Whizz® provides sales coaching, mentorship and sales consultancy.

•2020 and beyond, ... I've got new goals, plans and dreams, bring it on!

Why did I write this book?

Now you know a little more about me, I'd like you to know why I wrote this book. There are so many reasons that motivated me to put 'pen to paper', here's just a few:

• To help people.

• To help you! Yes, YOU. I'm in your head now and you're reading my words. What a privilege that is, thank you so much, I don't take this responsibility lightly.

• To share my knowledge and experience that I've acquired within sales over the last 25 years.

• To share with you a solid set of sales fundamentals and provide you with principles, key ingredients and tips & techniques to help you better succeed in sales.

• To help you with your emotional health & wellbeing.

• To persuade you that you 'can'.

• To encourage you to enjoy sales and 'high five and whoop' on a regular basis.

• To help you win and keep winning!

Writing a book has been on my to-do list for many years. I knew that writing a book required my sole focus and I knew that I'd need to dedicate myself and my time to this project. I've now been able to write this book because I've afforded myself the time to do so after the successful sale of my telecoms business in 2018.

I've employed, coached and mentored hundreds of wonderful people over nearly two decades. For me there is nothing more satisfying than watching my team flourish and succeed on the back of the advice and support I've given them, and now by writing this book, I'm here to do the same for you.

We might never meet or speak but I know for sure if you embrace the words I share, apply the methods I'll ask you to adopt and trust in me and more importantly yourself, you'll move forwards and fulfil your true potential.

As I'm literally writing these next few words on my computer, I'm thinking about the people that will be reading this book and here you are now reading what I've got to say. I'm going to pour my heart & soul into this book and provide you with every last ounce of the knowledge and experience I've acquired & gained over many years.

I'll write a number of **SALE ON SALES** books over the next few years, all on sales but each with a different flavour. This first book was always going to be on business sales.

Throughout this book I'll be asking you to tell yourself "I can, and I will", don't just say it, …feel it, own it and mean it!

It's important that when you've finished reading this book, you continue to tell yourself "I can, and I will" on a daily basis. It's this belief, attitude and mindset that will give you the strength, support & self-confidence to fulfil your goals.

Ok, let's move to the next section **ABOUT THIS BOOK** so you can get a flavour for the chapters included and the content you're about to read.

ABOUT THIS BOOK

Includes:

a) INTRODUCTION

b) WHAT TO EXPECT FROM EACH

CHAPTER.

a) INTRODUCTION

This book is now your business sales companion and will be a valuable resource that will help you reset and move forwards in your sales career.

We're going right back to basics in this book and building solid sales foundations so you will have the strength, support and confidence to build your sales career upon.

You've taken a big step already by buying this book, you're looking for some assistance and guidance from me and like a sales genie, 'your wish is my command', in fact 'YOUR WISH' is actually 'YOUR COMMAND'.

I want to get into your head and open your heart. If you allow yourself to be open minded and embrace my advice, I will help you succeed in sales.

Sales is fun and I want to encourage you to smile, laugh and enjoy each and every day. A 'high five and whoop' in sales is a wonderful thing.

This book is also a journey of understanding yourself better. You'll reflect on where you are now, where you've been and where you're heading emotionally, financially and professionally. With positive changes, you can fulfil your true potential and improve your emotional health & well-being. I can't stress enough the importance of getting your work-life balance right.

(Q) Have you got the balance right?

Sure, we'll talk about money, drive, ambition and success in this book, but your emotional health & well-being are important subjects too.

In **Chapter 9. EMOTIONS - Your mind and your heart** I discuss the importance of your thoughts and feelings. I intend to write a future book on this all-important subject, which I care deeply about.

I like to set good expectations, which is why I've set out what this journey will look like in **b) WHAT TO EXPECT FROM EACH CHAPTER**, so knowing in advance what this journey will look like for you, will help you navigate this book, immerse yourself in what I'm saying and embrace the changes that will be required so you'll get to the end of this book feeling more confident about yourself, your future and sales.

Setting good expectations is so important in sales. Your prospects & customers will reward you much more frequently if they are clear on what you're doing, how you're doing it and what you expect from them. I'll discuss this in **Chapter 2. SALES FUNDAMENTALS**

If you can add 'expect' to your 'want', you'll be on the right track for success. Of course, never lose the 'want' as that's the desire and drive that got you here and keeps you going each day, it's just important to want success so much that you 'expect' it, because you're doing the right things in the right way and you have complete faith in your own abilities.

I want you to be stubborn about your goals and flexible about your methods.

Are you currently working in sales and underperforming?

If so, I'm here to help you. Your current situation is just that, ...current. Yesterday does not have to define today, that's your choice. However, today always has the potential to shape your tomorrow.

If things are going well then repeat yesterday today and continue tomorrow. If things aren't going well, forget yesterday and use today as the kick start to a better tomorrow and beyond.

In sales, we remember the last 'yes' and work quickly towards the next one. Just ensure the gap between yes's isn't too far apart, if so, you need to reset to then move forwards.

If you've been working in sales for a while, then much of what I write might resonate with you. However, I'm expecting you to reset and move forwards, so open your mind and your heart as we need to rebuild those all-important solid sales foundations.

Are you new to sales?

If so, welcome to the wonderful world of sales! Are you enjoying it so far? It's important you learn the basics and build your future on solid sales foundations. Let's reset, backtrack a little and ensure you're on the right path for a successful sales career.

Are you wanting to work within sales?

If so, great decision. Sales can be fun, can be rewarding and can provide you a wonderful life. However, you need to prepare yourself for hard work and understand that you need to learn the sales fundamentals and continue to adopt them to give yourself the best opportunity to succeed in sales.

We're going right back to basics, so if you're not currently in sales, your journey will start in the best place with all the naivety, wonder and excitement that a new job in sales can bring.

In summary, I've written this book for YOU! so whether you're currently working in sales or not makes no difference to our journey together within this book. It's all about you and taking back control of your own destiny. So, let's reset, get you back on track and move forwards now, today! towards a brighter future.

b) WHAT TO EXPECT FROM EACH CHAPTER

Chapter 1. WHY SALES?

This is chapter 1 for a reason.

It really is important, essential in fact, that you understand and answer this question before you can reset and move forwards.

If you know why you're doing sales and you know what you want to achieve from sales, then you'll be in a much better position to succeed in sales. I know you'll be keen to get to the good stuff but please be patient with this chapter and start this journey with me by asking yourself, *why sales?*

Your answer will remain with you throughout your sales career.

Chapter 2. SALES FUNDAMENTALS: Principles, Key Ingredients and Tips & Techniques for successful selling

We'll go 'back to basics' in this chapter, so you can build your sales career on solid sales foundations.

For those already in sales, I'm sure you might already know some of these sales fundamentals. But do you still apply them to your daily role? have you ever applied them? have you questioned them? or, even rebelled against them?

If you can embrace and adopt the principles and key ingredients required, you'll be able to apply the tips & techniques I'll share with you to succeed consistently in sales.

Chapter 3. WORDS, TIMING AND TONE: What you say, when you say, how you say

This chapter continues the 'back to basics' theme in terms of what you say, when you say and how you say. Words, timing and tone are essential to your sales pitch and your interactions with prospects & customers.

You will close many more deals on the back of a well-constructed, well thought out and well delivered sales pitch.

Chapter 4. CLOSING: If you aren't closing then you aren't selling

This chapter is all about closing the deal.

In the end if you can't close then you aren't selling. If you aren't selling, then you aren't earning, and you won't be performing.

Your close starts at the very beginning of the customer journey and builds throughout your sales pitch. It isn't something that magically appears at the end of your sales pitch by surprise. If you're struggling to close deals, you'll find its all the things you've done or more importantly 'not done' beforehand that's the real issue.

A close is made on every sale, either you sell to the prospect and/or customer or they close the door on you.

Closing is infectious and needs to be relentlessly repeated.

Chapter 5. OBJECTION HANDLING: use their excuses to your advantage

This chapter will focus on your ability to overcome objections, which is obviously an important skill for you to have in sales.

If you're already in sales, I'm sure I could ask you to list a handful of regular objections you receive, and you'd happily list them. However, are you happy with the way you're reacting and responding to these objections?

In the end, it's all about results. Are you losing opportunities and/or deals because of the objections & excuses you're receiving and your inability to overcome them?

In this chapter, I'll arm you with the tools required to overcome objections & excuses and to use them to your advantage.

Chapter 6. INFLUENCER OR DECISION MAKER?

This chapter looks at the important roles both the influencer and decision maker will play in your sales process & pitch. Of course, the decision maker is the person you most want to be speaking to and negotiating with, however, when this isn't possible it's your ability to 'influence the influencer' that will be key to your success.

Chapter 7. RESEARCH AND STRATEGY: Knowledge with a plan of action

Research is essential! and must be a key part of your lead generation strategy and a key tool you'll utilise in gaining more sales. I can't stress enough the importance of research! I've used 2 exclamation marks already so I must be serious.

In this chapter I'll help you get one step ahead of the competition and more importantly one step closer to your prospects before you've even spoken to them.

If done correctly, you'll see instant results from the research you'll do. Good research will also enable you to have a better strategy in terms of how you'll engage your prospects & customers and how they'll engage with you.

Chapter 8. SALES ROLES: Telesales &Telemarketing, Field Sales and Account Management

This chapter looks at a few popular sales roles.

You might have done one, two or all of these roles? You might be currently working in one role and want to work in another? Or you might not yet be working in sales and you're undecided on what role might suit you best? There are more than subtle differences between these sales roles, in this chapter we'll discuss these in more depth.

You might find you're more suited to one of these roles and/or enjoy one of these roles more than the others? In the end, results will determine your sales role. Where are you wining? where are you performing? and where are you earning?!

If you have the ability to sell over the phone, book appointments, meet customers & close deals face to face and manage existing customers then you'll be adaptable to work in any sales environment. Add to this your ability to adopt the sales fundamentals you'll learn within this book and you'll be an all-round Sales Whizz®.

Chapter 9. EMOTIONS: Your mind and your heart

This is the most important chapter I've written in this book! For a self-help book on sales, that's a big statement to make.

Your emotional health and well-being need discussing, understanding and nurturing more than anything else.

Thoughts make things. Your happiness, your confidence, your mood, your drive, your passion, your ambition, your creativity and your commitment are all built from a combination of your mind, your heart and your emotions.

Your thoughts and feelings are very important, they need caring for with constant nurturing. Your thoughts and feelings have led you to buy this book and to read it. Your thoughts and feelings will determine how you read this book and what you do next.

I want you to dig a little deeper emotionally in this chapter and acquire a much deeper understanding of yourself. If you can tap into the wonderful resources which are your mind and your heart, you'll not only give yourself the best chance to succeed in sales but also learn to improve your emotional heath & well-being.

Chapter 10. WHAT NOW?

We'll close this book with a look back over the journey we'll have been on together over the past 9 chapters. I'll then have a final question for you, *what now?*

What you do NOW, TODAY and for the rest of your time in sales is so important. I'll explain why in much more detail within this chapter.

Also, our journey doesn't have to end, it's only just begun. When you've read this book, I'll be asking you to send me a personal message, as I want to know how I've helped you, as it will continue to quench my thirst for helping others.

Suggestion: Why don't you consider finding a colleague, friend or family member who is also working in sales, or wanting to work in sales and ask them to also purchase this book? You might find that it encourages you to converse with them, share your thoughts, feelings & opinions and keeps you focussed on the journey ahead. Or maybe you prefer to go this one alone for now and let your results be the thing that gets people talking?!…it's your call.

Ok, let's begin our journey together.

Chapter 1. WHY SALES?

Includes:

a) WHY ARE YOU WORKING IN SALES?

b) WHY DO YOU WANT TO WORK IN SALES?

c) WHY SALES FOR ME?

In this chapter, let's look at an important question to get you started on this journey with me, which is *'why sales?'*

Your answer to why sales? is essential. Maybe you're already clear on why sales? Maybe you're not? Maybe your reasons have changed over time? Either way, it's good to address or re-address this important question now before we start our journey together.

Important: If you're currently working in sales, after you've read section **a) WHY ARE YOU IN SALES?** please continue to read section **b) WHY DO YOU WANT TO WORK IN SALES?** *Don't skip this section!* As I want you rewind back to the time when you weren't in sales and wanted to start your sales career. Are you as keen and eager now as you were back then? Have you been given bad sales advice over the years? or, maybe you've inadvertently given bad sales advice yourself? When you've read section b, you'll appreciate why I'm asking you these questions.

If you're not currently working in sales and are considering a sales role, you must still read section a, *don't skip past this first section!* I need you to appreciate that if you don't start your sales journey building those all-important solid sales foundations, you'll more than likely end up underperforming in the future and reaching out for help.

a) WHY ARE YOU WORKING IN SALES?

If you're currently in sales, then the chances are you're under performing and you've realised you need help to succeed.

Maybe you're close to giving up? Or, maybe you're performing ok but need help to push on further? It's never too late to press the reset button, but the longer you've been in sales the more you'll need to dig deep to change your mindset, attitude and sales beliefs.

You'll also need to re-evaluate your sales pitch. Your words, timing and tone are the key ingredients to a successful sales pitch. Your sales pitch will need resetting with a new understanding and a fresh perspective.

I'll explain this in more detail within **Chapter 3. WORDS, TIMING AND TONE: What you say, when you say, how you say.**

Maybe you've never really asked yourself why you're in sales?

Maybe the reasons have changed over the years?

Maybe you fell into it?

Maybe you've been doing it that long you think this is all you can do?

Maybe you've been successful, but this has changed?

Maybe you're up and down throughout the year and can't maintain a successful consistency?

Maybe you're just a little lost and need some guidance to find the path of success?

Maybe self-doubt has kicked in and you're thinking of giving up?

Maybe you've started cutting corners, letting people down and you know your sales are tainted with bad sales practices?

You'll have your own reasons I'm sure as to why you're in sales and your current situation is just that, 'current'. Yesterday does not have to define today, that's your choice. However, today always has the potential to shape your tomorrow.

So WHY are YOU in sales?

…. please take a moment to think (…. I can wait)

Money?

I'm expecting this to be top your list, is it?

Commission is what differentiates a sales role from any other. It's your opportunity & ability to earn a commission that sets you apart from a non-sales role. However, *(Q) Are you earning a commission regularly? and is it enough for you?* I'm guessing not which is why you've purchased this book and why you've made the decision to improve yourself and push on in your sales career.

Commission is a wonderful incentive in sales, however, there are many other rewards you'll receive from working in sales and money should not be the only reason of course. The money you earn needs to be wrapped around the other benefits you'll receive from working in sales.

Other than Money, why are you working in sales? Here's a few suggestions I'm sure you'll include:

Interacting with people

Talking to people on a daily basis is a wonderful thing, it really is.

Sales provides you an opportunity to interact with a wide variety of different people. These interactions can be fun, interesting and challenging.

I've always tried to ensure that when I'm interacting with prospects & customers, I'm rememberable and I brighten up their day. Brightening up someone's day will more than brighten your day too, and the people around you. It's a win-win.

Targets

The only people who don't like targets are those that often fail to hit them.

(Q) How often do you hit your targets?

Sales is all about targets, if we hit our numbers, we expect a commission and/or bonus.

Targets keep us focused, driven and competitive.

If your boss is setting targets that are achievable and that will reward you for hitting them, then great. If they're not achievable or are not providing the level of financial incentive to warrant the time and effort to hit them, then you either need a conversation with your boss about addressing this or you need to find a new job.

I've always set my own targets too and so should you. What's stopping you from setting your targets that bit higher? I've always thought that if I was a long jumper and the world record is 8.95 meters, I'd train to jump a bit further, that way if I fall a little short I might still have beaten the world record as I've been focused on a target a little further than what was required.

However, you might find that you actually hit the higher number because that's what you've been focusing on and working towards. Now is the time to negotiate a stretch target with your boss, to ensure you're suitably rewarded for overachieving within your targeted period. This will also prevent you from having to 'sandbag' your numbers until the next month or quarter.

Challenges

Sales often provides many challenges to overcome.

You'll have challenges such as targets and performance KPI's.

You'll have sales challenges in terms of how to attract and interact with new prospects.

You'll have the challenge of persuading your prospects & customers to buy your products & services.

You'll also have internal challenges, in terms of keeping your confidence, drive and focus where it needs to be to perform at your best.

(Q) What do you find most challenging about sales?

Problem Solving

Your prospects & customers will often have problems that require solving and your products & services might provide the solutions.

You might find that although your products & services provide solutions, your prospects & customers aren't yet aware of the problems, it's your job to highlight these to them.

Competition

All the very best salespeople are competitive, I'm sure you are too.

In fact, you'll find that with every winner there is a competitive streak that is a key ingredient and attribute in their DNA.

Sales is a competitive environment and competition is everywhere. You're competing with other salespeople within your business and other salespeople that are interacting with the same prospects & customers as you. However, most of all you should be competing with yourself. If you ensure that you are the best you can be and you set your own bar higher than any of your competitors you'll win, and often.

In the Whitney Houston song 'One Moment in Time' there is a line that says, 'racing with destiny', a beautiful line. You really are in a race with yourself, keep up, get ahead and ensure that you create & shape your own destiny.

(Q) Are you destined for greatness?

Recognition & Praise

We all like to hear "well done" & "thanks" once in a while and receive a pat on the back, or a high five.

When was the last time you felt appreciated by your boss, a customer or a colleague?

Sales provides plenty of opportunities to be recognised & praised by your employer, customers and colleagues. You might also be recognised by your industry or by the media.

For me, the best recognition is the one you give yourself, tell yourself much more often that you're doing well (when you're doing well) and give yourself a pat on the back on the days when no one else does, when no one else knows or when no one else cares.

The Buzz

Sales provides a great buzz! Whether it's the high energy of a busy sales office, the chase of a prospect or the acquisition of a new customer, the emotions before, during and after are incredible.

That's where the high five and whoop comes in, that feeling you get when someone high fives you or you high five them is great as it symbolises a positive action, followed by a 'whoop' and you know life is good.

It's your job to create the buzz when necessary, it's good for you, your colleagues, your prospects and your customers. Everyone benefits from the aura and positive energy you'll transmit.

Q) Do you create a buzz in sales?

Personal development

Sales is a brilliant environment for personal development.

You'll get out of sales what you put in. If you put your heart and soul into sales and adopt a core set of sales fundamentals, you'll develop skills and knowledge that will benefit you throughout your sales career.

Personal development isn't a short-term goal, it's a lifetime of understanding yourself with the ability to identify, improve, learn and nurture those areas that either need attention, understanding or support.

You've purchased this book which is evidence enough that you want to improve. Good for you! keep it going.

Career progression

Sales is a great job for career progression as you'll get noticed if you're selling and performing.

You'll be noticed not only by your employer but by the employers you're selling into. If you're on social media and you're sharing your successes, you'll be noticed by a wider audience too.

Of course, not everyone wants to be a manager or run their own business, but what you need to understand is that by sharing your experience, knowledge and skills to others is a valuable tool and commodity.

Where do you want your career path to take you?

Manager, Director, CEO, or is it eventually a life outside of sales? Maybe it's the same job as you're doing now, with more money? or with a better work-life balance?

As I said earlier, career progression isn't always about having a manager's title or being self-employed, it's how, when and why YOU want to progress.

The best advice I can give you is to keep selling! and smashing those targets, everything else in sales will follow.

Don't wait for opportunities, seek them out.

Dream big! You can be, do and achieve much more than you realise.

Focus on your goals. 'Thoughts make things', visualise your ideal future career path and then set small manageable goals along the way to meeting your objectives.

Be flexible to change. The dreams, goals and career plan's you have at 19 years old will often be different at 25 and 35 and so on. Just because you might change your path or change the time frames doesn't mean you've failed, it means that rather than thinking 'life has got in the way', you realised that 'life' encapsulates work & home and you've embraced a happy work-life balance.

Tell yourself on a daily basis "I can, and I will".

In summary, If you like speaking to/helping people, if you like targets, if you like solving problems or overcoming challenges, if you like working on your own or the buzz of a busy office, then great! but you obviously don't need to work in sales to achieve what you like or want. There's plenty of jobs outside of sales that can give you all of this and more.

Sales provides a commission that wraps around what you like and what you're good at. In sales you expect to be paid a commission for the products & services you sell.

You don't just speak to people, you persuade people.

If you hit your targets, you expect to be rewarded.

You expect to be paid well for your ability to help people, solve problems and overcome challenges.

Knowing your true worth and expecting to be paid well is an important trait to have if you want to succeed in sales, especially if you're the one creating the buzz and making all the noise with your sales.

Just reaffirm the important message to yourself that you're in sales to earn MONEY!

You need to be realistic; you know yourself better than me. If you know you won't dig deep, if you know you don't and won't embrace change, if you know you're just too stuck in your ways, then hit the stop button not the reset button. However, if you're willing and able to dig deep emotionally, embrace change and give yourself a kick up the backside when and if required, then good for you, ...let's do this!

If you'll go above and beyond to achieve your true potential, then high five and whoop! you've already hit the reset button, good for you!

I need you to keep an open mind and read this book with a renewed sense of optimism, with a belief that this book can be the spark that relights the fire inside you.

Now to reiterate, if you're already in sales, you must read the next section. Much of what I'm about to say, I'd like to have had the chance to say to you back when you started in sales. However, I've got the opportunity now and more importantly so have you.

If you're not currently working in sales, then reading this first section has just given you a flavour for why others are in sales, so the question to you is….

b) WHY DO YOU WANT TO WORK IN SALES?

Is it the commission? …

If so, good for you! Money should be at the forefront of every salespersons mind. This should be an important reason for you wanting to do sales, but as you've just read in the previous section, it shouldn't be the only reason.

Your suitability to sales such as your personality, your intelligence, your drive and ambition might be what's led you to want to work in sales, but it'll soon be money that'll be the driving force in your sales career if you're to be successful.

Maybe you know someone in sales and want to give it a go?

Maybe someone told you they think you'd be good at sales?

Maybe you currently work in a non-sales role and are fed up watching people earn more money than you and get more recognition than you?

Maybe you've read books or watched films or YouTube video's and it's inspired you to give it a go?

Maybe you want to run your own business and sales is the start of your journey?

…You'll have your own reasons I'm sure.

Whatever your reasons, let me be clear. Just because someone tells you that you would be good at sales doesn't necessarily make them right. Are they qualified to say this? Sure, they might be in sales themselves, but beware.

Just because someone tells you that you won't be any good at sales doesn't make them right. If these people aren't in sales themselves, ignore them! What do they know? If they are in sales, then you'll listen to their reasons (if they have any) and you might agree with some of what they say.

However, whether you do or don't do sales is on your terms and you'll never know unless you try. The world is full of doubters and naysayers, try to avoid them. If you want it enough, you'll find a way if you adopt the correct sales fundamentals.

You're about to take your first steps into sales and the biggest pitfall is listening to bad advice. If you know what to listen out for, you'll soon know who to listen to and who to avoid. You'll also know when to press the mute button on the noise around you as sometimes you can be overloaded with advice which then becomes about you dissecting people's opinions.

One of your greatest assets as a new salesperson is your naivety. You're pure, you're open minded and you're not tainted by any previous sales experiences.

You're going to face obstacles and challenges and you'll take a few knocks here and there, but hey ho, that's life and that's experience, it'll do you good in the long run.

You must avoid sales advice from people not in sales, what do they know about sales?!

You need to surround yourself with successful and positive people. Negative people will bring you down, they'll make you doubt yourself, make you cautious and they'll quash your ambition.

Beware of taking advice from people in sales that aren't hitting targets and don't earn much. Why would you want to say, act and do as they currently do? Sure, they might provide you some valuable advice and steer you away from a few pitfalls but be careful as too much of this advice might provide you with fear, caution, doubt and negativity. These people will often also play the blame game and tell you it's never their fault. If they turn things around and start performing consistently sure you can then encourage more of their advice as they'll provide a valuable insight to their ups and downs and how they turned things around. The fact they are now winning will allow you to feed off their newfound confidence and positivity.

You can read all the books and watch all the films and YouTube videos you like, but until you're in a position where you're doing sales yourself, you'll never know how it feels, and if you 'can'. That's why, after reading this book, for those that are still excited and ready to pursue their sales career I'd suggest reading this book again once you're actually doing sales, as it'll give you a whole new perspective, understanding and appreciation of yourself, your role and sales.

The emotional side of sales is so important. Your heart and your mind are important things to understand, they have personal settings that need programming and constant nurturing. I'll dedicate a future book to the subject of emotional health and well-being, it's so important and I care deeply about this subject.

There are many films that give sales a bad name and give a false impression of the reality of this wonderful world. They often promote a 'get rich quick' culture and regularly portray bad sales practices and mis-selling.

In **Chapter 2. SALES FUNDAMENTALS: Principles, Key Ingredients and Tips & Techniques for successful selling** I'll talk about good and bad sales practices as there's a huge difference between the two. Stay true, stay honest and always stay on the good side of sales.

Beware of taking advice from people in sales that haven't got a commission structure. Sure, they might be on a high basic (and that's their incentive) because they regularly hit targets and so commission isn't applicable. Although, even these highflyers will have stretch targets, bonuses and additional incentives, it's what a Sales Whizz® would do. However, if this isn't the case they're not in sales, they'll tell you they are but in my opinion they're not. For me, a salesperson is someone that is paid a commission and/or bonus (often in addition to a basic wage), for the products & services they sell.

Beware of taking advice from a salesperson that has a commission structure and target but can't explain in a few minutes the structure of how their commissions and targets work, as it will often mean they aren't performing, aren't achieving and almost certainly aren't earning!

Salespeople that are underperforming and not earning commission often have little understanding of their targets and incentives as they've rarely hit or achieved them. Those that are aware often see their targets as unachievable and commission as nothing more than a hopeful want and certainly not a regular expectancy on their pay slips.

And finally, what I'm also advising you is to stay away from the people that choose to cut corners and talk B.S. They are a serious danger to your sales career!

In summary, let me be clear, if you aren't prepared for hard work, willing to dig deep emotionally and put yourself out there, then stop now! keep doing what you're doing and leave sales to those that will do what it takes to succeed. If you want to succeed in sales, you need to respect the process and be realistic in your initial goals before shooting for the stars.

For you to truly know if you're able and suitable for a life in sales you need to start from a blank canvass and allow yourself to build from solid sales foundations. If you're prepared and willing to do these things, then you'll give yourself every chance to succeed in the wonderful world of sales.

In sales you're ultimately judged by your ability to sell.

For those people already working in sales, I'm sure you've just read this section and some things resonated for you.

(Q) If you could go back to when you first started in sales, what would you change?

Look, you obviously can't go back in time and make different choices. However, you can affect your future in a positive way by the decisions & actions you make & take today! So, use all those yesterdays as an important resource in how and why you'll reset today and how and why you'll shape tomorrow and beyond.

c) WHY SALES FOR ME?

It's only fair I answer this too, as I've asked you.

The 19-year-old, 23-year-old and 43-year-old Dean would all say Money! I set out to become a millionaire and I chose sales to help get me there. Having achieved my initial goal, I can now reflect a little further on why sales? …

Sales brings out the best in me.

Sales requires my focus, my drive, my confidence, my ambition, my desire, my honesty and my integrity. I've never lost sight of those key ingredients.

Sales enables me to hunt, requires me to be persuasive and encourages me to compete with myself and my competitors. We've all evolved from hunter gatherers, it's these primal instincts that I enjoy.

Sales provides me with positive fulfilment and a regular sense of achievement, as I'm often winning.

There's nothing better than earning a good living on the back of providing a good deal and great service.

Sales requires me to set targets and provides barometers that allow me to measure my success. It's a continual cycle, when one target period is over, it's quickly on to the next one. I love the relentlessness of sales, it's addictive.

I've often told myself "I'm only as good as my last sale" as it's kept my eyes on the prize and has maintained my focus, drive and ambition.

I love the buzz of a sales team, the banter and the 'high five and whoops' I give and receive.

Sales allows me to set my own goals and shape my own destiny.

Sales has enabled me to coach and mentor many people that I've employed over 20 years in business, and this continues today with my new business Sales Whizz®.

Sales is my passion and it's afforded me a wonderful life.

Sales is in my heart and is obviously in my name too!

Now we're both a little clearer on why sales? let's continue our journey together.

Chapter 2. SALES FUNDAMENTALS: Principles, Key Ingredients and Tips & Techniques for successful selling.

All successful salespeople will have built their careers on solid sales foundations. That's certainly the case for me.

These solid sales foundations are built over time and are acquired 'on the job'. Knowledge can of course be acquired by books, videos and training courses. However, experience, understanding and appreciation can only be gained by 'doing' sales yourself.

What many successful salespeople have in common is the fact that it's not all been plain sailing and a continual bed of roses. We've all had up's and down's and have hit a few bumps in the road emotionally, financially and professionally to success along the way.

Every successful salesperson obviously started somewhere, and whether this 'somewhere' was the bottom step of the ladder or a little higher, we've all shared a belief that things will improve, life will get better and that we 'can and will'. It's this belief, drive and optimism that shapes our futures. It's certainly shaped mine and I'd like it to shape yours too!

What all successful salespeople will agree on is that understanding, embracing and adopting a core set of sales fundamentals is the key to a successful sales career and is the strength that supports those all-important solid sales foundations. It's your ability to sell that will ultimately determine how successful you are in sales

You'll need to be persuasive, persistent and relentless, amongst many other things.

Your sales career will be shaped by your experiences, both the high's and the low's. Sales will challenge you and ask you plenty of questions. You'll need to overcome these challenges and find many of the answers yourself. That's what human beings do, we adapt, we evolve, and we learn to find a way.

I can obviously only write about my own experiences within this book and share with you my own personal sales beliefs. However, of course you're unique and have your own personality and your own personal hopes and dreams. You'll soon find your own way and develop your own style, and so you should, you're not a robot and you must be yourself.

The plan is for you to use this book to support the solid sales foundations you build your sales career upon.

Now, before we move on, let me be clear on an important subject I spoke about in the last chapter. Whether you're already in sales or not, you must know and understand that there are good and bad sales practices, an ethical way and a non-ethical way, a right way and a wrong way.

If you're already working in sales, maybe you know people that have adopted bad sales practices? or maybe you've adopted them yourself either knowingly or inadvertently?

If you're wanting a long and successful career in sales, it's important to make the decision now, early doors, that you won't adopt bad sales practices. Tell yourself that you'll do it properly or not at all.

By understanding what good and bad sales practices look like, you'll know how to best conduct yourself and also what signs to look out for so you can ensure you don't let bad sales practices creep into your job and affect your sales career.

Let's look at two brief examples of good and bad sales practices. Stick to these principals, live by these morals and reap the rewards that the law of attraction will provide you. Hopefully, your moral compass always keeps you on the good side of sales.

Good sales practices (brief example):

You've provided products & services where you've not cut corners, you've remained professional throughout and the promises you've made you can back up and fulfil.

You've put the customer first and you've understood their needs and requirements.

The products & services you offer meets the customers' requirements and you've been thoughtful and diligent during the process.

The customer will most likely recommend you to others based on the wonderful service you've provided. The customer is also likely to renew or reorder based on these positive experiences.

The commission you'll make on the back of these sales will allow you to feel accomplished and grateful to the process.

You'll sleep easy at night knowing you've done the right things in the right way.

You'll most likely receive recommended sales because of your good sales practices.

It can take a long time to build a great reputation, but it can be lost in a heartbeat. Once you've started to build and grow your great reputation, you'll soon find that you'll attract new customers and sign plenty of business on the back of it.

Repeat business and recommended sales are the fruits of your labour.

Bad sales practices (brief example):

You've cut corners, made false promises, over sold and under delivered.

You've put yourself first and not the customer.

You've been unprofessional and either haven't understood the customer requirements or haven't bothered to listen.

You've been thoughtless and lazy throughout the process.

You might close a few deals, but if you think for one minute that the customer will recommend you to others or will renew and reorder, you're wrong.

The commission you'll make on the back of these sales is tainted and depending on the severity of your bad sales practices, obviously at risk of being taken back by your employer (and so it should be!).

You'll eventually be found out for what and who you are!

It's not ethical, it's not sustainable and it's just not right.

I'd rather make half the commission with integrity than double the money without. Just by having this mindset will soon deliver the results you want and expect.

Remember, the people you're selling to have often experienced the good and bad salespeople. ***Disrespect buyers at your peril!***

Below is a mix of 75 principles, key ingredients and tips & techniques for successful selling.

Combined, these sales fundamentals will give you the solid sales foundations for you to build your sales career upon.

Now, some of the things I've listed below might seem obvious and sound like common sense, especially if you're already in sales. Well, here's the thing, they are! you might just have lost sight of them or have never considered them.

In order to reset, you need to go back to basics and rebuild your sales career on those all-important solid sales foundations. Often the problem is that you're so busy rushing around in your daily life that you rarely slow down and take stock of the basic sales fundamentals.

Over time many things will change in your life and in your sales career, but these sales fundamentals won't. These trusted allies will support your sales career through the up's and down's and will be a beacon of hope to guide you to success and happiness.

Don't lose sight of them and don't ignore them. Embrace them and continue to adopt them.

So, let's get to it, I've not placed the list in any particular order as all are individually important, but combined they are super powerful!

I've also placed questions with a *(Q)* alongside some of these sales fundamentals. If you're already working in sales, I'd like you to answer these questions yourself now and continually throughout your time in sales. If you're not currently working in sales, you'll need to answer these questions when you embark upon your sales career.

Of course, these sales fundamentals include all sales roles. So, if you don't currently make outbound calls, or, you don't meet customers face to face, still read through all 75 of these principles, key ingredients and tips & techniques as they'll give you not only a good overview of sales, but will also benefit you if you decide to switch roles in the future. In **Chapter 8. SALES ROLES: Telesales & Telemarketing, Field Sales and Account Management**, I discuss these roles in more detail.

1. KNOW YOUR PRODUCTS & SERVICES

It's essential that you have a good knowledge of the products & services you're selling. Immerse yourself in them and get interested in them.

Develop a thirst for knowledge about your products & services.

Ask questions to as many people as possible, especially those that use them, 'those' being your customers.

I've heard salespeople over the years say, "the product sells itself". NO! you sell the product and you'll need to sell yourself and your business too. If the product sold itself it would get on the phone, attend meetings and close deals for you. Of course, that's not possible. You're the voice of the product, the rationale, the clarity and its greatest advocate. You champion the product and receive an incentive for doing so.

Speak to people within your business about your products & services, especially people that don't work in sales. You'll be surprised by how much knowledge can be acquired by speaking to your customer service team, service engineers, account managers etc. These people can often provide you with the reassurance and testimony required for you to truly believe in your products & services. You'll soon start to use these reassuring tones in your sales pitch.

Your colleagues might also flag up issues or open your eyes to things you were not aware of in relation to your products & services and more importantly how these have affected customers. As a team you collectively have a responsibility to ensure you're offering the very best service in relation to your products & services.

Read as much marketing collateral as possible.

Log onto your own company website and/or the various manufacturers and/or suppliers you use as there's usually a treasure trove of information available.

Keep abreast of industry news, subscribe to newsletters and magazines and look over social media regarding your products & services.

Stay up to date with current affairs that affect your business which might then affect your products & services.

The best advice I can give you when it comes to reading any form of marketing collateral or doing this type of research, is to do it in your own time, ideally from home. The conditions at home are more suitable for learning and you can then ensure you use your 'work time' for driving sales!

(Q) What more can you learn about your products & services?

2. KNOW YOUR FEATURES & BENEFITS

(Q's) Do you appreciate and understand all of the features & benefits that your products & services provide? and do you regularly highlight and promote them to your prospects & customers?

Not all sales are closed on price alone, far from it. Of course, if you're offering what's required and you're cheaper then great. However, some prospects & customers might pay more, for more. What I mean by this is that your prospects & customers might pay more for your products & services than they are currently paying if there are additional benefits to their business such as increased productivity, improved efficiency, reduced waste, better customer service, the list goes on.

The features & benefits of your products & services are essentially the 'bells and whistles' that will either meet or exceed your prospects & customers' requirements.

Features: Are the characteristics of your products & services.

Benefits: Are the reasons why your prospects & customers will buy your products & services.

Your job is to sell the features to your prospects & customers and highlight how they will benefit from them.

The more benefits provided the more likely you are to close more deals.

Your prospects might not currently use the products & services you're offering and so it's your job to ensure that you can highlight how your products & services will benefit their business. Your features & benefits will facilitate this.

3. KNOW YOUR TARGET AUDIENCE

Now for some, the products & services they'll sell might have mass appeal and suit a wide range of prospects & customers. For others, there will be a target audience and possibly a niche market.

You might find that although your products & services have a mass appeal, your business suits a certain customer dynamic, be that SME or Corporate, or industry specific. If so, embrace this and target prospects where you know you'll get your foot in the door and are likely to receive opportunities to sell to them.

When you're selling products & services to a target audience you need to understand that audience and consider their wants & needs and problems & solutions.

Market research to your target audience is an important thing to do. You'll gain a deeper understanding of how they are thinking, how they are feeling and more importantly how, when and why they are buying.

Existing customers are a great resource to acquire further knowledge from, so continue to speak to them after you've sold to them.

(Q) What's your target audience?

4. KNOW YOUR PROSPECTS & CUSTOMERS

It's essential for you to know your prospects & customers.

People buy from people, so it's important to know as much about your prospects & customers as possible.

You'll notice throughout this book I say **'prospects & customers'**, it's important for you to understand the difference between the two, a prospect is not a customer (…yet.)

I get annoyed when I hear a salesperson call a prospect a customer. You have to earn the right to call your prospect a customer, close your deal and your prospect will be a customer. Sure, they are potential customers for you, and they might be customers of your competitors, but if you get the terminology right, you'll ensure that you don't jump the gun and get ahead of yourself by calling them a customer too soon.

Of course, if you're working as an account manager the likelihood is, you're often selling to existing customers. Some of these you will have acquired yourself and others you'll have inherited from others within your company. These are your customers of course, but you'll appreciate they are your competitors' prospects.

You might have existing customers that become new prospects in terms of new products & services that they don't currently purchase from you. However, they're still existing customers, which of course provides you an advantage.

Stick to the principle that prospects aren't your customers (…yet).

I'll continue to say **prospects & customers** throughout this book, as I appreciate that you might be selling to new prospects, existing customers or both.

Also, 'prospects' & 'customers' can be people and/or the businesses they work for. For the purposes of this book I'll mostly refer to prospects & customers as the people, the influencers and decision makers. Of course, the businesses they work for are your prospects & customers too.

Q) How well do you know your prospects & customers?

Sure, you'll need to research and understand the businesses they work for but the person you're speaking to directly is the most important person to know. Research plays a key role in this, as there is much you can learn before you've even spoken to your prospects & customers. The research you'll do before speaking to your prospects & customers will be one of the key reasons you'll not only get to speak to them but also build trust, empathy and mutual respect.

In **Chapter 7. RESEARCH AND STRATEGY: Knowledge with a plan of action** I discuss the various resources and techniques available to better know the people you're speaking to and the businesses they work within.

With the vast resources available today such as social media, there is no excuse not to have a mini portfolio on your prospects & customers.

Of course, the best way to get to know people is by speaking to them and building a rapport. The best way to start this relationship is by being welcomed and liked in the first place.

With the right research, you can get to know the people you're speaking to (or about to speak to) and start to paint a picture of who they are and what makes them tick. Within minutes it's possible to know their age, where they live, if they are married, if they have kids, if they have a pet, what school they went to, their academic achievements, the sports teams they support, the jobs they've had, the music they like, the sports they play, where they've been on holiday, where they are going on holiday, what they did last weekend, what they are doing this weekend, what their political views are, what they like, what they dislike, what they care about, …the list goes on and on.

This research is simply using what's already out there in the public domain, much of (if not all) what they have put out into the universe themselves. It's what they want you to know!

If your prospects & customers have private social media accounts and you've already spoken to them, connect with them with a view to then doing more research and possibly communicating with them on these platforms.

It's now your job to use this information to help you build a rapport with your prospects & customers. Find the mutual interests you have with them and find the topics that will best encourage good conversation, good debate and empathy.

You must also ensure that you continue to paint this picture of your prospects & customers when you speak to them and/or meet them and update accordingly as the real world is often different from the digital world. You'll obviously learn new things from your prospects & customers when you personally interact with them, this learning often comes from your ability to ask good questions and to listen accordingly.

I'm amazed more salespeople aren't doing much more research in their own time. All that time spent on their mobiles and on social media could be used towards acquiring more prospects, building relationships and ultimately selling more in work time.

(Q) How well do you know your prospects & customers?

If your prospect is an influencer and not the decision maker, then it's essential the influencer is championing you when presenting your proposal to the decision maker. In this scenario, it's important to know your decision maker too, even if you'll never meet them, as there's much you can benefit from and use to your advantage.

If you will be presenting your proposal directly to the decision maker, then you need to do the same research as you did for the influencer.

5. INFLUENCER OR DECISION MAKER?

You need to establish from the start of your conversations with your prospects whether they are the decision maker or not. You need to know who will be making the final decision and who is influencing this decision. **Chapter 6. INFLUENCER OR DECISION MAKER?** Is dedicated to this important subject.

6. RESEARCH

As you've already read in this chapter, research is a key ingredient in sales and is essential if you want to have a long and successful career.

I can't stress enough the importance of research. **Chapter 7. RESEARCH AND STRATEGY** is dedicated to this subject.

The most successful salespeople do much of their research in their own time. Don't allow research to be an excuse as to why you're not on the phone or in front of your prospects.

It's one thing having good quality research information but another knowing what to do with it. In chapter 7, I also discuss the best strategies for how to use your research information to get you in front of more prospects, build a greater rapport with them and get more deals over the line.

Good research takes you well beyond simply knowing more about your prospects & customers personally, it extends to the company they work for, the industry they work within, the customers they supply and so much more.

Good research will also require you to know who the current supplier is and the journey they've been on over the years re: your products & services.

As I say, I'll pick this back up with you in much more detail in chapter 7.

(Q) Are you doing enough research?

7. SAY NO TO SALES SCRIPTS

(Q) Do you read from a sales script when you're on the phone?

If you do, let me persuade you not too. You'll sound like a robot and your personality won't shine through.

A script means you've already pre-determined the call and you won't interact with your prospects efficiently and effectively. You'll stop listening to your prospects and if you're interrupted, you'll be waiting for where you left off in your script rather than reacting to what was just said or asked. You've got 2 ears and 1 mouth for a reason, so learn to zip it as and when required.

You need to engage your prospects within the call and if your questions and prompts are good, you'll listen as much (if not more) than you'll speak. You'll learn much more too, and you're much more likely to build rapport and progress the call in a positive direction.

You should use prompts (bullet points, reminders…) to ensure you are talking about what's important, what you've researched and what will progress your call to a successful outcome. You'll kick yourself if you come off an unsuccessful call realising you hadn't mentioned some valuable info that could have benefited you and your prospects.

Even when using prompts, you need to be flexible and ensure you don't just force feed information to your prospects. Let the call flow, steer the conversation when required towards the points you want to make and don't order your points in such a way that you have to follow that order. Some points will be made organically within your conversation, some will be prompted, and others will be cleverly manoeuvred by you. Some points might need to be left for another time, as you either thought it wasn't appropriate, wouldn't add value, or is best kept in your back pocket for another time and opportunity. All these decisions can only be made whilst you're actually on your sales calls.

As I discuss in **Chapter 3. WORDS, TIMING AND TONE** you're in control of what you say, when you say it and how you say it.

A good way to practice this, is to make a list of 5 important headlines or messages you'd like to discuss on the call and 3 important questions you'd like to ask your prospects, where the answers might get you the info you need to move the call to the next stage or to a successful outcome. Then use your conversational, sales and listening skills to facilitate this. It's your ability to listen and react that is the important message here.

As I mention within this chapter **8. CREATE A KNOCKOUT SALES PITCH** and in **Chapter 3. WORDS, TIMING & TONE**, you'll need a knockout sales pitch to best deliver your points and acquire the answers you require.

If you use a script, you'll ensure 3 things:

1. Your prospects will stop listening.

2. You'll learn nothing new because YOU aren't listening.

3. You'll be so repetitive, you'll soon become bored and frustrated with your daily routine and this will be evident in the delivery and success of your sales calls.

As a sales coach, whenever I'm asked to help write a sales script, it's a definite NO! However, what I will do is help construct a knockout sales pitch, based of course on what you sell, and focusing on:

• Words, timing & tone.

• Open & closed questions.

• Research & strategy.

The key is to then use this knowledge and these skills & techniques to construct a knockout sales pitch, without having it written within a script.

Of course, I appreciate you might be reading this, and your employer adopts a sales script policy and encourages you to use one. If so, I'm happy to contact your management team to persuade them not to, and to work with you all on creating a new sales culture within your business. Or, ask them to purchase a copy of this book and consider a new perspective.

A sales script is not a recipe for success.

Every call & every prospect is different and that's the fun. It's your ability to listen and react whilst at the same time having a structure and plan with your sales pitch that will determine your success when making outbound calls in sales.

8. CREATE A KNOCKOUT SALES PITCH

Note: I say pitch, NOT script! I'll discuss this in much more detail in chapter 3.

Your sales 'pitch' is the approach and strategy you'll use all wrapped up by your choice and understanding of your words, timing and tone.

Your sales pitch isn't a script and has no restrictive order to it. Each call is different, and each prospect and/or customer requires something different from you too.

Although at the very core of your sales pitch is a solid structure in terms of your approach and strategy, you'll still have in your 'sales locker' the ability to pitch to your prospects & customers in the way that is best suited to them. Not much will change in terms of the words you use, but your tone and especially your timing will adapt according to each individual call or meeting.

Adapt your sales pitch from time to time but don't give up on it too soon. Remember the last 'yes', and if this wasn't too long ago and you are fairly consistent in hitting your targets then you can tweak and improve your sales pitch but don't give up on it just because you've hit a bad run. Equally, you need to know when your sales pitch needs a major overhaul, if the gap between yes's has been a while, if you're not hitting your targets and you don't have confidence or faith in your sales pitch then change it. You might find that it was actually nothing to do with your sales pitch, but more to do with your confidence in it. Either way, it's all about results.

If you're finding new opportunities and acquiring new business on the back of a good solid sales pitch that you're comfortable with and believe in then great, the yes's you receive will be the best judge as to whether you have a decent sales pitch or not.

(Q) Have you got a knockout sales pitch?

9. SELL YOU AND YOUR COMPANY

(Q) How often do you sell the benefits of you and your company to your prospects?

Some of the key benefits you're selling aren't just related directly to your products & services. You will also be promoting the benefits of your company and highlighting the benefits of you and your team.

All successful salespeople know and play on the fact that people buy from people. You are a key reason as to whether someone buys the products & services you offer, so sell yourself.

Tell your prospects about yourself. Share with them your interests, talk about your family, your background, your charity work etc.

We've all got a story in us, something that tells someone all they need to know about your character, your feelings, your passions or your drive. Whatever the story, if it's true and if it's you, then share it.

Paint them a picture of you. Now, let me be clear, I'm expecting you to be the person in your painting. Don't give a prospect the impression you're anything other than you actually are, as you'll soon get found out. If you paint a picture of yourself that isn't actually your current reality, but the reality of a person you aspire and want to be, then make the changes necessary to be a better version of you now, today and moving forward.

You need to know your company inside and out. You'll know the basics, sure. But appreciate that the agreements your prospects will sign is with your company and not you. Again, you're painting pictures of your company with a view to building trust, confidence and reassurance with your prospects.

Your prospects will want to know that your company is successful, secure, reliable, efficient and most of all the right choice for them. A great way to cover this is by explaining to your prospects why YOU work for your company. Let's face it, if you're good at sales and have a great reputation and track record of success, you choose where you work and how you work. You've chosen your company and they chose you for a reason, this is as good a reason as any for your prospects as to why your company is the right choice for them too.

Speak to other employees in your company, especially outside of sales such as customer services, marketing, IT and accounts as it's essential you know what your sales processes are, as you'll be explaining (and selling) this to your prospects. You'll be promoting (and selling) the benefits of these people & teams too, especially if these teams will be involved with your prospects, during or after you've been successful in securing new business with them.

When researching your sales processes, don't just list them, walk a sale through yourself from start to finish, touch and feel it each step of the way. I can't express strongly enough the value of walking a sale through from start to finish. I can assure you; you'll learn plenty of things you didn't know along the way. Let's face it, your commission is often based on the successful implementation of your products & services so you need to know the processes and stages involved that can support or affect your ability to earn money!

Setting good expectations is important too. Your prospects need to know what your sales processes are, each step of the way. Your sales processes might be one of the things that helps you get your deals over the line! so sell the benefits of this.

Sell your speed and efficiency, due diligence and those little extra's that highlight that your company knows exactly what it's doing as a business and appreciates what customers want and need. Customers expect to be well looked after, so ensure you live up to and supersede these expectations. I discuss setting good expectations a little further on within this chapter **43. SET GOOD EXPECATIONS**

From time to time, ask your colleagues what they're working on, what's going well and what pressures they're under. Work with and support your colleagues. You're selling you and your business, so you need to ensure those around you are singing from the same song sheet and supporting you, especially if your colleagues are customer facing.

You need to know your company inside and out, do the same research on your own business that you would for your prospects. You might never use all of this information, but you'll be informed and empowered if you're asked questions by your prospects, or, you want to include some key info within your sales pitch.

Consider that your prospects might have done their own research on your company, you don't want them to know more than you, do you?

Knowledge really is power; it'll energise you and will empower you to sell you and your company whilst at the same time selling your products & services.

10. GET YOURSELF IN THE ZONE

It's important that you get yourself in the right frame of mind when doing sales.

Getting your mind and your heart 'in the zone' is essential when it comes to the practical side of sales, the 'doing'.

A positive mindset is so important in sales. When you say, "I can, and I will", you're sending out a positive message to the universe. It's this belief, attitude and mindset that will give you the strength, support & self-confidence to fulfil your goals.

Think of an athlete, a long, triple or high jumper. Often before they start their run they whip up the crowd with a hand clapping gesture, the crowd acknowledge this and slowly clap back, this builds to a crescendo and you can see the affect it has on the athlete, they are now 'in the zone' and focussed on the task in hand, they start their run and the jump follows.

In sales, it's the same thing, before you hit the phones or attend your first meeting you need to get yourself 'in the zone' and focussed on your goals and objectives.

In **Chapter 9. EMOTIONS: Your mind and your heart** I discuss various techniques to help you 'get in the zone' and best prepare for a life in sales.

11. LEAVE IT AT THE DOOR

Of course, this is easier said than done but you must learn to leave many of your 'day to day' issues at the door when working in sales.

Now let me be clear, I'm talking about day to day stuff here and not emotional health issues that affect your well-being.

Day to day issues are often the kind of things that life throws at us, and often do get resolved fairly quickly. They are often just mini blips or bumps in the road, no real drama or cause for concern. If it can be left at the door then do so, in sales (at work) there's enough to think about. Unfortunately, your personal issues will still be there waiting for you at the end of the day and for as long as they take to resolve.

You need to determine what you can leave at the door and what is rooted much deeper within your mind and heart and requires help & support to understand, solve, resolve, forgive or forget. We all carry emotional baggage, and of course some have heavier loads than others.

The contents of your emotional baggage are of course personal to you, and the weight of this baggage can only be determined by you. However, talking to someone can often lighten the load. In **Chapter 9. EMOTIONS - Your mind and your heart** I discuss how talking to others (either to friends or professionals) really can help. A problem shared is often a problem solved.

You can't perform successfully in sales whilst trying to juggle your personal issues and challenges at the same time.

I have so much respect for people that ask for help. It all starts with you, if you know you're struggling and know you're suffering then please understand you don't need to know why, before you ask for help. You might have no idea why you're feeling like you do, or you might think you know why and can't do anything to change this.

Of course, there is a level of mental strength required to perform at your best in sales, and there are times where you will have to push on and push through life's battles.

If you know you can't leave it at the door, then don't, seek help & support. If you can leave it at the door, then do so.

(Q's) Are you taking care of yourself, your emotions and your well-being?

12. STAND UP WHEN YOU'RE ON THE TELEPHONE

Q) Do you stand up when you're on the telephone?

If your role involves making outbound or receiving inbound calls, then you need to stand up (if you're able to) when speaking to your prospects & customers. Standing up when on a telephone call has so many benefits.

When you're on your feet you're more alert and responsive. Whilst sitting down your posture is more relaxed and it's easy to be distracted by things on your desk or PC.

If someone called you to complain you'd soon stand up, why? it's because you want to be on your toes and ready to react. You might feel defensive and want to adopt a defensive position. The point is you stood up to be at your best.

When we speak to friends and family we often walk around whilst on the phone, this is because we want to focus all our attention to the person we're speaking to. Well, your prospects & customers deserve and require the same respect.

13. SMILE AND DIAL

This might seem obvious, and it is! However, you need to ensure that you're doing this.

You can't switch your smile on and off in an instant or switch your mood from bad to good when the telephone phone rings.

Smiling releases neurotransmitters called endorphins. Endorphins are triggered from movements of your muscles in your face, such as a smile. Your brain then interprets the smile and releases these chemicals.

Encourage yourself to smile often. Get your mind and your heart in the zone and use visual and audio stimuli to get you feeling happy, positive and ready to win.

Consider how many emoji faces your own face might portray each day, there are so many to choose from. They might include happy, sad, angry, confused, laughing, worried or frustrated. You're in control of your feelings and your mood and your face will often express how you're feeling, unless you're faking it. If you're faking it, then there will other things to address before the smile has the affect you require.

I'll discuss this in more depth in **Chapter 9. EMOTIONS: Your mind and your heart.** When speaking on the telephone, your smile will be transferred down the telephone line to your prospects & customers, they will hear it in your voice, and it will be infectious.

If your prospects & customers are already smiling, then great. If they are not, you've got more chance of them smiling back if you're smiling. Your persuasive tones & words and your enthusiasm will all be coming from a happy place.

I often hear salespeople that (although they might be happy), sound miserable because they are being too professional or too insecure of rejection.

If you're happy, be happy! It's a simple as that. Your prospects & customers will often join you in your happy place and often reward you for it.

I discuss this further in this chapter **68. BE HAPPY**

If you're not happy, then you need to find that happy place in your mind and your heart. If this is easier said than done, then you need to address your emotional health & well-being and help yourself.

Smile and dial and see the difference it makes.

14. POSITIVE SPEAK, POSITIVE TONE

(Q) Who is the most positive person you know, and why?

In **Chapter 3. WORDS, TIMING AND TONE** I'll discuss with you the importance of positive words and a positive tone. It's that important it required its own chapter!

It might seem obvious, but you must ensure you use positive words with a positive tone continually. Not just within your sales pitch, but at all times.

Positivity is an attitude; it's a mindset and it supports your belief when you say, "I can, and I will'.

I discuss this further within this chapter **59. BE POSITIVE**

15. DON'T SAY 'COLD CALLING'

Don't ever say 'cold calling', it creates a real negative connotation of the true art form you adopt each day, called sales.

Ban it from your vocabulary and stop others from saying it too.

Encourage positive speak, you're lead generating and you're getting your positive message out there. Your timing couldn't be better, your prospect might just be in the market to buy your products & services. If so, that's not cold, it's positively warm.

Positive speak, positive thoughts and a positive attitude will often get you over the line. I've never made a sales call thinking I was searching for cold prospects, as they rarely are. The only thing that might be cold is you, get on your feet, get warm, get prepared and get calling your prospects!

Your prospect works for a business that is up and running and so by its very nature active and warm. They are buying and selling as part of their role and you simply want a piece of the action.

Look at it like this, if you're cold (on a cold day) and you step into an unheated swimming pool, you'll feel cold, right? If you're warm (on a warm day) and you step into an unheated swimming pool, then the water will often feel colder as your body temperature is further away from the water temperature. As some salespeople hit a wall or face rejection, they lose confidence and their demeanour portrays all things cold. No wonder, these people call it cold calling. It's as if they think the rejection won't be as bad if they call out cold and speak to cold prospects, as the gap between temperatures isn't that wide. There's not as much shock to their system and life simply stays chilly, flat and unsuccessful.

If you're cold in your sales approach, you'll only ever receive a cold response. You need to be warm and positive in your call, the prospect is more likely themselves to be responsive and warm if you are. Keep the temperature between you and your prospects at a nice warm manageable gap, I expect you to always be a little warmer as you're working harder and pitching.

I think some salespeople assume so much that the prospect is cold, they either work twice as hard and end up sounding desperate or fake, or, they work less and sound cold themselves. Either way, it's a recipe for failure.

As you'll read in the next section, you need to expect that many of your prospects will be receptive & warm and that you'll be well received by most. Sure, you'll need to warm them up further and you will if your your sales pitch moves through the gears nicely. If your research is good, then you'll have plenty of things to speak about that will continue to warm them up.

Keep yourself at a nice toasty temperature and allow yourself to increase the temperature (your tone) a little throughout the call if required.

Your prospects really are warmer than you think. So, ban yourself and those around you from saying "cold calling", you're a sales magnet and you're on fire and ready to generate some great leads from some great prospects. Lead generating is an attitude that requires positivity and a 'want' to get on the phone in the first place.

16. EXPECT TO BE WELL RECEIVED

You must expect to be well received. You can't fake it; you need to believe it. If you expect to be well received, you often will be!

(Q) Do you expect to be well received?

Why wouldn't you be well received by your prospects? if you're good at your job (and you have a knock out sales pitch), you've got wonderful products & services to offer (that can make a positive impact to their business) and you can brighten up their day a little (because you're smiling and dialling), then many of your prospects will appreciate you calling and assisting them.

Have you considered that many of your prospects work in environments that also have sales teams and people just like you, doing the same things as you? We're all one big community of people that are buying and selling our mutual products & services to each other.

The next time you're lead generating, consider what I've just said and if you come up against a prospect where you're not being well received and you feel the call is heading towards a swift end, ask them how their own internal sales team operates and are they prospecting today just like you. If so, then you're doing exactly the same as them!

Keeping those wheels of industry turning. Ask them to give you a break, a chance, an opportunity.

If you expect to be well received, you often will be!

17. INVEST IN THE HEAD OF FIRST IMPRESSIONS

The head of first impressions, often called the receptionist is a really important person within any company. I've employed many heads of first impressions over the years and I've been clear to emphasise that they are often the first impression someone will have of our business.

When you're lead generating you'll often speak to this person before anyone else within that company. You often want them to transfer you to someone else, point you in the right direction, help you with fact finding and provide information to support your future communications with your prospect.

There's so much reliance on the head of first impressions, so respect them, charm them and most of all don't pitch them! They aren't there to be sold to.

You'll often speak to the same head of first impressions on your future calls, so the more you can get to know them and build your own rapport with them the better.

In **Chapter 8. SALES ROLES** - I discuss how to best invest in the head of first impressions in more detail.

18. NEVER APOLOGISE FOR CALLING

Why would you apologise to your prospects when calling them? Are you really sorry? of course you're not.

I've heard salespeople say, "sorry for disturbing you" or "sorry to bother you". If you think you're disturbing or bothering them, then you will be, and you'll encourage your prospects to feel disturbed and bothered.

It's like asking your prospect "have you got a few minutes to spare?", this will often encourage a no. For a start you gave your prospect an easy way out, and also why would anyone have time to spare if they don't know why they're giving it, and to who.

Presume your prospect is ready and able to take your call and they often will be, they often are! If you think you need permission for a few minutes with your prospects you won't get it. Presume you have permission and presume they have the time. If the prospect hasn't got any time for you, you'll soon be told so anyway, so assume the best scenario.

Remember, all prospects will be thinking 'who are you and what do you want', not in a negative way, it's just the natural position they'll adopt.

In **Chapter 8. SALES ROLES** I discuss that your first 30 seconds has been given to you for free, by every prospect. You don't need permission and you don't need approval. From thereafter, it's up to your prospect as to how much longer the call continues and how successful you are on the call. You'll now need further time credits, chapter 8 explains all.

19. THE NEXT 5 CALLS

In brief, this 'mindset' highlights why you need to ensure your sales pitch is delivered consistently each and every time with high energy and positivity, whilst at the same time not letting a negative call affect the next call/calls.

'The next 5 calls', will be a mix of good and bad in terms of your prospect's attitudes and responses to you.

The point is to expect that you will come across people who will try and shake your confidence, try and test your resolve and try and ruin your day. If you allow these people to succeed, you'll take these negative emotions into the next call/calls and subsequently it will affect your sales pitch and encourage a negative response from what should have been a positive response from a positive prospect.

The power of this mindset works both ways. Take a positive response into the next call and you're much more likely to receive a positive response, even from what might have normally been a negative prospect. That's why you should always remember your last 'yes' and take the energy of this into each and every call.

Expect that you will come across plenty of happy and positive people who will lift your mood, make you smile and make your day.

Every 5 calls you make is a beautiful mix of different people with different responses. These differences are what keeps sales fun, challenging and rewarding.

20. DIAL QUICKLY AFTER A GOOD OR BAD CALL

Telesales is a numbers game, always will be!

You'll reduce these 'numbers' with successful calls of course and with good research too. If your talk time highlights long and successful conversations then great, that's the plan. If your talk time highlights short and unsuccessful conversations, then you need to look at your sales pitch and strategy.

It's important to dial quickly after a good or bad call. You must not spend too long pausing and thinking about either before getting back on the phone.

After a good call, why spend too long patting yourself on the back, you're good at your job and that's what you're being paid and incentivised to do. Sure, go get that high five and whoop as it's important to you and everyone around you, but get back on the phone and repeat your good work quickly. There will be plenty of time at the end of the day, when you hit your target and more importantly when you pick up your pay slip to congratulate yourself.

After a bad call, why beat yourself up, question yourself or punish the prospect in your mind. You'll achieve nothing other than making yourself feel bad and you'll have wasted your valuable call time. Sure, get it off your chest quickly if you have to, but get your mind and heart back in the zone and get calling those positive prospects.

Remember, a negative thought can only hurt you. You expect to be well received and you often are. However, you also expect that from time to time you'll speak to negative people, "whatever!" move on, stop being so sensitive and don't let anyone shake your confidence or test your resolve.

Remember the last 'yes' and know the next 'yes' is on its way.

Telesales and telemarketing will always be a numbers game, so get dialling! In **Chapter 8. SALES ROLES** I discuss this and more in greater detail.

21. BREAK THE ICE

You will build a greater rapport and learn more about your prospects, when the conversations you have with them are unrelated to the actual reason you're speaking to them. Talk about something current, or something the prospect will respond or react to, your research will obviously help!

Be an opportunist. If you're in a meeting, look around you and start a conversation based on what you see or hear. Look out for the prompts and play on them.

If you're on the telephone use your research to break the ice and talk about something you know will encourage a good response. Breaking the ice, is ensuring there are no awkward silences, avoiding pointless small talk or getting straight into work talk. It avoids an interaction that is formal and has no flavour or personality.

If you break the ice well and you engage with your prospects on a friendlier level, you'll often maintain that level/tone throughout your calls and/or meetings and throughout the quoting process.

Get them on your side, dare to be different and be liked.

(Q) How do you break the ice?

22. INVEST IN YOUR VOICEMAIL

(Q) Do you put thought and effort into your voicemail messages?

Just because you might not listen to voicemail messages yourself doesn't mean your prospects don't or won't.

You need to be ready to leave a voicemail message if your prospect doesn't answer and they have a voicemail facility on their direct dial or mobile. Your voicemail message needs to be original and needs to encourage your prospect to call you back.

Now here's the thing…always leave a message but then tell yourself not to rely on it to do your job, as often it won't. It'll encourage you to call your prospect back and chase them up.

Now for some, the fact they haven't got hold of the prospect means that at best they'll leave a message saying "Hi, this is who I am, this is why I'm calling, please call me back". You'll sound robotic and unenthused; you'll rarely get a call back with a message like this.

Have you ever considered what a wonderful opportunity you have with a voicemail message, you've got the prospects full attention (if they listen to their messages of course) and they've got one of their ears allocated just for you, so get into their mind and heart and encourage them for a response. Intrigue the prospect and most of all dare to be different. If you don't receive a response, you'll at least leave a positive impression for your next call.

There's no excuse for not leaving a brilliant voicemail message, you've got plenty of time when you're not at work to prepare. Limit what you say to no more than 30 seconds. Also, ensure that you only provide your return number at the end of the call, and repeat your name too. Just because you said your name at the start of the call doesn't mean the prospect remembers it, as they didn't have any reason too then, now they've listened to your message and might want to call you back they'll need a reminder. This is the same for your return number, why would the prospect want or need to write it down any sooner than at the end of the call. The last thing a prospect will want to do is listen again to your message just to get your name and number.

If you're calling their mobile phone and the number to call you back on is the number you're calling from then mention this in your message, it saves them having to write it down. You can also use the missed call trick; I'll explain how in the next section.

I always use 'thanks in advance' at the end of my voicemail message as it's being presumptive that I'll receive a call back, and I'm expecting a call back too.

My advice is to prepare a few different voicemails and see which ones work for you. Think of your voicemails like fishing bait on a hook, see which fish bite and use that bait for a while. When the fish stop biting change your bait and try another.

Have fun with it and dare to be different!

23. MISSED CALL TRICK

If you're calling a new business prospect on their mobile or DDI and they don't answer, try the missed call trick (from time to time) and call back 20 seconds later, your prospect might think the call is important. Of course, to you it is!

Of course, if you work from a dialler, or as I like to call them a 'call efficiency system' this might not be possible for you?

If the call isn't answered on the 2nd attempt, then leave your voicemail message.

However, your prospect might be expecting a call? or think the call is work related? maybe it's the kids school calling? or family or friends? you get the gist.

Don't ever fear annoying the prospect and receiving a negative response. If you do this, you'll encourage that reaction. It's not your fault they didn't recognise the number and thought you might be someone else. Expect to be well received and play the percentages.

Always use caller ID as you'll often find a withheld number is rarely answered, and there's no possibility of a returned call.

Some prospects will call you back before they've even listened to your voicemail message, when they see a missed call number on their screen. Some prospects might listen to your voicemail message and use the missed call number as their reminder to call you back, rather than make a note of your number (if it's the same one).

Of course, always ensure that the data you're calling meets all your company compliances such as GDPR, TPS etc.

24. INVEST IN YOUR EMAILS

Emails are an important tool in your sales arsenal.

Again, just like when I told you not to rely on a voicemail message to do your job, you must not rely on an email either. Your job is to speak to your prospects, not to send loads of emails in the hope that you get a response. Let email support you, not work against you.

Remember, like I said with voicemail, you've got an opportunity for that brief moment to get into your prospects mind and heart, they're reading your words in their heads, just like you are now reading my book, what an opportunity!

There will be opportunities before, during and after speaking to your prospects where a well-constructed and thought out email will assist you in receiving a response, an opportunity and a closed deal.

The content, subject line, structure and tone of your email combined with the time of the day you press the send button can make a huge difference to your overall performance within sales. I could write so much more about this important subject, in fact as I write these words, I've decided that's exactly what I'll do! it'll probably be a book based on sales tactics and social selling.

Some prospects might prefer to communicate via email rather than speaking to you. If this is the case, embrace it. Of course, you'd rather speak to them but if they are responding to your emails and you're moving things forward, great. When you do speak, you'll find the tone of the call is always better. Of course, most people also use email via their smartphones and tablets, so consider that not everyone is stuck behind their PC in the office when receiving and sending emails. This has the added advantage of your prospects & customers using email in their own time outside of working hours. For some, this will mean they are more receptive, and able to communicate with you when they aren't in the office.

Top tip:

People often forget to do things and often require a reminder, so this strategy helps you get what you want when expected.

Let me create a scenario:
You've emailed your prospect and asked them to send you some information and you receive a reply from them to say they will send it tomorrow. Don't acknowledge this email (saying 'thanks' etc) until tomorrow! as it will then also act as a subtle reminder for them on the day they said they'd action your request!

If you think your reply can act as a subtle reminder and not responding immediately won't do you any harm, wait until the time you know will have the best impact before replying. You can use this strategy with text messages too.

25. WHAT DO YOU WANT TO ACHIEVE FROM YOUR CALLS OR MEETINGS?

Be realistic, you'll know yourself what's likely and unlikely to achieve from your calls and/or meetings, so your objective should always be to ensure you get the bare minimum with a view to moving forwards and progressing things. Anything more than this then great but focus on the things you're looking to achieve and secure them.

If you're looking to arrange a meeting, then focus on this and get that date in the diary! Sure, you'll be pitching and saying what's required to get the meeting whilst at the same time acquiring important information that will assist with the meeting and quoting process but don't talk yourself out of a meeting by asking too much or talking unnecessarily and being inpatient to close a deal.

Be patient, if you're more likely to receive an opportunity to quote a prospect and more likely to understand their requirements and build rapport & trust by meeting them, then do what's required to get that date in the diary.

If your interactions with your prospect will all be via telephone and your prospect isn't giving you the buying signals required, then arrange another call, buy yourself some time, do more research and rethink your strategy.

It's ok to get mini wins, if they're often and they build and lead to a successful outcome. It's knowing what a mini win looks like before a call or a meeting and knowing when you've 'won' for that call, that meeting or that day without pushing your luck.

Of course, there's nothing better than pushing your luck from time to time and taking a chance on the big close early. It will pay off sometimes, but if the percentages say small and steady often wins the race, then that's what you need to do.

For some, you'll be selling products & services that don't require multiple calls or meetings and for others it's rarely a closed deal on the first call. These factors will determine your expectation levels and sales strategy.

Each of your calls and/or meetings will be different and will be at a different stage in your sales pitch and process. Consider with each call or meeting what is the least and most that can be achieved and set yourself an expectation to achieve something from this next interaction.

26. IT'S NOT ABOUT YOU, IT'S ABOUT THEM

A prospect doesn't want to hear you babble on talking about only you, your business and your products & services! but of course, that's what you want to do.

You'll be able to tell the prospect all this and more within a two-way balanced call, where you're asking the right questions and listening & reacting to the prospect's prompts. You need to learn to ask questions that then encourage and enable you to say what YOU want to say, after your prospects have themselves responded. You can control the subject matter and the flavour and tone of your conversations if you learn this technique, and it won't look like it's all about you.

Do your research, knowledge is power! You'll have shared interests with your prospects & customers, both personally and professionally, so use this to shoehorn in the points you're looking to make.

Ask your prospects for their views on a particular subject and on the back of their answers you can then express the views & points you were originally looking to make. It's a simple technique but an effective one.

Keep your prospects engaged and involved in your conversation. People like to talk about themselves! Their lives, work, interests etc, so encourage your prospects to do just that, it doesn't matter what the subject matter, if they are speaking then you'll soon join in. Flatter them, encourage them and compliment them, you'll be amazed how often they will do the same for you.

Once again, research is key here. The more you know in advance, the easier it is to prompt and encourage great conversation.

Let's say you want them to know you supply a well-known business, as it will raise & enhance your profile to them. The easiest way to do this is to research if they supply any well-known businesses themselves, then comment on this before making the synergy that your company also supplies well-known names, brands etc.

If they've done charity work comment on it, you can then share your charity work too.

If their company has won an award, comment on this before then letting them know about your company awards.

If they've received great testimonials, comment on this before informing them that likewise you've been acknowledged and recommended too.

The key here is to ensure that you first show interest in them and ensure that when you make your own points, they naturally feed & flow into the conversation. You don't want to be too obvious that your agenda all along was to make your own points.

Practice makes perfect, you'll know in advance what you want to tell them and what you think will be valuable information for them to know. Your research will provide you the touch points to facilitate this, so you can prepare in advance the questions you'll ask, the points you'll make and the information you'll provide them.

Of course, you're still fact finding yourself and acquiring information that can assist you, so ensure you're also asking fact finding questions, listening and taking notes. You're also building rapport, so ensure you remain interested in your prospects. Sometimes, it's the smallest detail that you remember and comment on in future interactions that can make the greatest impact.

27. USE FIRST NAMES NOT SURNAMES

When talking to the head of first impressions only use first names, not surnames.

As you've read in section **17. INVEST IN THE HEAD OF FIRST IMPRESSIONS** it's important to appreciate that if you want them to transfer you to someone else, point you in the right direction, help you with fact finding information and provide you information to support your future communications with your prospects, they are more likely to do this if they think you know the prospect and they don't assume you've never spoken to them before.

As an example, if you're calling and wanting to speak to Ryan Smith, then ask for Ryan.

If there is more than one Ryan in the company, you'll be asked which one, you can then of course say Smith, with a tone that suggests you knew all along which Ryan, but you of course appreciate there's two of them.

Of course, if the person you're calling has a more common name like John, you're more likely to be asked which one. You might choose beforehand to say John Smith, especially if you've done your research and know or assume there are other John's in the business. Or if you've done your research, you might know what department John Smith works, so you can say "John in accounts" for instance.

When asked for your name only say your first name followed by your company name. To use your surname implies that you've never called before and the prospect doesn't know you. Why reveal this fact when it's not required.

If I was calling an existing customer, I'd ask for my contact by first name and say it's Dean from Sales Whizz®. So, when I'm calling a prospect why would I say anything different.

In **Chapter 3. WORDS, TIMING AND TONE** and in **Chapter 8. SALES ROLES** I discuss in greater detail how to best approach, engage and interact with the head of first impressions.

(Q) Do you already do this?

28. PRACTICE BEING AD-LIB

The best salespeople have the ability to sound ad-lib and off the cuff when in fact they are totally rehearsed and diligently prepared.

What you say on a daily basis doesn't change too often and the main ingredients of your sales pitch remains fairly constant. What will change is the way you deliver your sales pitch and who you deliver it to.

As you read in section **7. SAY NO TO SALES SCRIPTS** if you use a script you'll sound like a robot and you'll stop listening.

The true art of your sales pitch is to sound unscripted and not robotic and over rehearsed. However, of course, there will plenty of opportunities to actually be ad-lib and to go off-piste, which is why you need to be ready for when these opportunities arise. The ability to be creative, engaging, fun and interesting within your conversations is important, so much so that you should practice. You can (and should) practice being ad-lib in your own time.

Ask a colleague or a friend to choose a letter of the alphabet and then start a conversation with them about a topic of their choice only using the letters of the alphabet in sequence, starting with the letter they initially chose.

The rules are that you must use the letters of the alphabet in order following on from the starting letter chosen and the first word you speak must begin with the next letter each time. The conversation needs to be coherent and must make sense like any normal conversation should. The conversation ends when you arrive back at the starting letter.

The point here is that you are preparing yourself to think on the spot and to be creative whilst at the same time following a particular narrative. You're going to get curve balls thrown at you by your prospects & customers and you need to be ready to respond and able to get the conversation back on track in a natural way.

You'll be surprised by just how much better you are within your conversations.

When you're being ad-lib, you'll be creative and when you're delivering your sales pitch you won't sound so scripted and over rehearsed.

Some of the best stand-up comedians, are brilliant at going seemingly off-piste and sounding ad-lib whereas in reality they tell the same stories and deliver the same jokes & lines night after night. The real genius is that they make the audience feel like this is the first time for them & for you. However, every decent comedian has the ability to actually go off-piste and be ad-lib especially when they are being heckled, they simply have a comedy brain to get them out of the situation. You have a sales brain which allows you to build rapport, engage, be liked & persuade even when you're not talking about your products & services.

You're always selling, because you're selling yourself.

29. OBJECTION HANDLING

(Q's) What objections do you often receive? And how do you overcome them?

You're going to come up against objections in sales, that's part of the game. In **Chapter 5. OBJECTION HANDLING**, I discuss this in greater detail. I'll also share with you how you can actually use their excuses against them, as you'll find many objections are actually excuses.

Your prospects & customers will disagree, disapprove and push back from time to time, that's ok, that's their job as buyers. It's your job to find out why they object and discuss what's led them to this view. It's also your job to provide facts and to encourage and/or persuade them to change their mind, view and opinion.

They might not understand, even though they think they do.

They might not have received all the facts.

They might have received all the facts but have used them to conclude the wrong outcome.

Their opinion might be influenced by someone else.

They might have an agenda.

They might be right; you won't overcome all objections.

Preparation is important in sales, and you can prepare for many objections you'll receive in advance of your calls and/or meetings. Sure, you'll receive new ones (curve balls), that's the fun and challenge of sales. You'll think on the spot and you'll overcome some and acquiesce on others.

30. OPEN AND CLOSED QUESTIONS

Asking great open and closed questions are essential tools in your sales armoury.

In **Chapter 3. WORDS, TIMING AND TONE** I discuss open and closed questions in greater detail, to ensure you have a better understanding and appreciation of your questioning skills.

There are times when you simply require 'yes or no' answers from your prospects & customers and times where you need much more information from them.

Understanding and adopting a great questioning technique will improve your sales pitch, keep you in control of your calls and/or meetings and get you over the line closing many more deals.

31. THE YES LADDER

If you can get your prospects & customers to say 'yes' a few times during conversations they'll be much more likely to say yes, when you really need one and you need them to be agreeable. This technique is often referred to as the 'yes ladder'.

Having used this technique on numerous occasions, I can vouch for its effectiveness.

The initial yes's you're looking for don't need to be anything to do with your products & services and don't need to be relevant to work. The plan is to build from fairly mundane topics (chit chat talk) building to yes's that will provide more substance and will be more meaningful as you head towards what you're looking to accomplish, such as an invite to quote, setting a meeting date or closing your deal.

Try it yourself with friends and family, engage in a conversation and encourage them to say yes. Comment on the weather, something in the news or whatever you choose but keep getting them to say yes, to nod and to be agreeable.

Reverse it, can you imagine if all you did was encourage no's, after a few no's you'd imagine someone with their arms folded getting ready for the next no, they'd be so disagreeable.

Use the 'yes ladder' to your advantage and get them nodding!

32. DON'T BE INSECURE

Insecurity is best friends with self-doubt, avoid these emotions.

Insecurity will make you question everything:

Why hasn't the prospect called me back?

Does the prospect like me?

Will the prospect say no to my deal?

Can I do this job?

Am I good enough?

(Q) Do you ever ask yourself any of these questions?

If you're secure with yourself, you'll never ask yourself these questions. If you like yourself, if you're confident in your own abilities and if you know you can do the job then trust me (and more importantly yourself), your prospects will have the same opinion and belief in you.

The insecurities of prospects & customers not calling you back or delaying their decision re: your proposal are things you can always affect if you know how, I discuss these techniques in the next few chapters. If it's a good deal and you've done your job properly, then more often than not you'll receive a call back and receive a yes.

If you encourage a no, or a negative response you'll often attract one, the law of attraction often works like this. If you think 'yes' and are confident enough to know you'll win many more deals than you'll lose, then you'll win and often too.

Much of this comes down to your mental strength too.

33. MENTAL STRENGTH

Throughout this book, I talk a lot about mental strength, emotional health & well-being.

Mental strength is a key ingredient in sales.

Mental strength is the power behind many of things discussed in this chapter. It all starts in the mind, 'thoughts become things'.

A strong, confident, positive and focused mind is a sure way to success in sales. You need to control negative thoughts and encourage positive ones. Don't indulge a negative thought, challenge it and counter it with a positive thought. 'I can't' really should be 'I can', in fact it should be 'I can, and I will'.

A negative thought can only hurt you. Don't worry about out things you're not in control of, if you can't affect the outcome and it's out of your control, then why worry about it? What will be will be. You'll often find you needn't have worried anyway, so why did you put yourself through all of that misery?

In the end the only person you can rely on in sales, is yourself. So, make sure YOU are in the best condition to help yourself succeed. If you're mentally strong and have a heart filled with ambition and drive, you'll succeed in sales if you adopt the correct sales fundamentals.

However, you can learn all the sales fundamentals you like, but if you're not mentally strong enough to overcome the hurdles and challenges of sales you'll fall at the first hurdle often. In **Chapter 9. EMOTIONS: Your mind and your heart** I discuss mental strength in more detail, focussing on your emotional health & well-being.

(Q's) Are you in the best condition to succeed in sales? Or, do you need to work on your mental strength?

34. OPINIONS NOT JUDGEMENTS

It's healthy to have opinions and even healthier to change them.

Judgements should only be made based on facts, and even then, you should be flexible to change, as we often rarely have all the facts.

In this section, I'm focusing on the opinions you have about yourself and the judgements you might make about your own abilities in sales.

I recall a number of people I've employed over the years that had never worked in sales before. After only a day or two they had decided they couldn't do telesales and things wouldn't improve, even though I'd asked them to have opinions but not make judgements. I reiterated to these people why I'd employed them, why I thought they had the qualities required to succeed in sales and why if they give up now this early, this trend might follow throughout their life. I reiterated that I employed them because in my qualified opinion, they had the qualities to perform in sales, and I explained why. I also reiterated that I wouldn't be making any 'judgements' on them so soon, I'd keep an open mind and wait until they'd settled in and had time to receive more sales coaching from me before expressing my opinion on their sales abilities.

Each and every one of these people made the decision with my help to turn their judgment into an opinion and were open minded to the possibility that things might get better. Things often improved and quickly too, and with my guidance, support and coaching they realised that their initial judgement was wrong. This I'm sure, would have been an important life lesson for them too. You've heard the phrase 'don't judge a book by its cover', well that's true about you. Don't judge yourself by past failures, or where you've previously given up so easily. Life isn't about the sprint, it's a much longer race than that. Life is more like a marathon that requires you to run the whole distance at a consistent pace.

35. DARE TO BE DIFFERENT

Stand out from the crowd, and don't be the same as everyone else.

I've never been trendy, and I've never wanted to follow the crowd. That doesn't mean I don't understand and appreciate the benefits of trends and the advantages of a popular crowd or large following, especially working in sales. What I mean is, I will 'dare to be different' when and if required.

Sure, there are plenty of things you'll do each day because they work for you and provide you with positive results. However, have you considered that you might get in front of more prospects if you stood out a little more from the crowd.

Your prospects & customers are being approached by other salespeople some of who might be standing out from the crowd? This is a competition, don't ever forget that. Sometimes it's the subtle differences that can make the greatest difference.

It's your job to find out what 'the norm' is and work out how best you can stand out from the crowd. Look at what your colleagues do, look at what your competition does and adapt accordingly, whilst still giving yourself the edge and that extra sparkle.

The point here is that if you're not being noticed enough, not getting your foot in the door enough and not getting your deals over the line enough, then 'dare to be different'. I say dare because it takes bravery & courage to try new things, often out of your comfort zone. You'll try a few things before you hit on ways that get you noticed more, get you in front of more people and get more deals over the line. That's the fun! Dare to be different.

(Q) Do you stand out from the crowd enough?

36. VISUAL TARGETS

Visual targets are the best way to ensure you're keeping yourself on track, motivated and moving forwards.

If your targets are visual then everyone can see them, this can add a little more pressure if you're not performing but at the same time it'll highlight to you and everyone else when you're winning and when you're hitting your targets. You'll encourage plenty more 'high fives' from your colleagues and hopefully your boss!

You can display your targets however you think best. A whiteboard works well, you can write down your targets in numbers and track accordingly. You can break your numbers down by the hour or by the day, whatever works best for you.

You can draw actual targets, such as the red and blue targets you see in archery etc and each time you close a deal or book an appointment etc, you can draw an arrow smashing the target. The point is, at the start of your targeted period (be that a day, a week, a month or a quarter) it's good to have a visual representation of your targets and where you are in relation to them.

Put yourself out there, put your targets out there and most of all put your performance levels out there. Be confident, you've got this, and you'll show yourself and everyone else that you're a winner!

Write in big letters at the top of your whiteboard, 'I can, and I will'.

I discuss visual targets & motivation in more detail in **Chapter 9. EMOTIONS: Your mind and your heart**

(Q) Are your targets and performance levels out there for everyone to see?

37. DON'T SHOUT FROM THE ROOFTOPS WHEN YOU WIN BUT STAY QUIET BEFOREHAND

If you're prepared to let everyone know what your targets are and highlight how you're performing in relation to them, then take it a step further.

Challenge yourself and others on a daily basis to push further and win.

If you work in an environment with others doing the same job, then get the competition going. Tell them you're going to WIN today, sell more products & services, book more appointments, increase more of the KPI's…whatever it is, put yourself out there and set the challenge.

You're not doing this in an arrogant way, you're doing it to challenge yourself more than anyone else, but also when you win, it will be so much more special and rewarding because you predicted it.

It's an attitude and drive that says, 'I can, and I will'. Sure, you might lose from to time, but I bet you'll sell more on that given day than you would have done. So, you're still winning, you just didn't win the race that day.

It's these extra driving forces we all need in sales. If you suffer a loss, then everyone will of course see this, hey ho, you're going to lose sometimes. You might get some office banter and you might energise your colleagues in sales, especially those that are competing with you. However, you'll be back tomorrow, working harder and smarter than ever to reclaim your position as top dog!

The point here is that if you're prepared to share your targets and your performance with your colleagues and the universe! When you win, it'll mean so much more because you didn't hide from putting yourself out there, you said you'd win, and you did!

There is nothing worse than a salesperson that loses (often) and says nothing, but only shouts about it when they win (rarely).

38. VISUAL MOTIVATION

Following on from the visual targets section, let's look a little further at visual motivation. Visual motivation is a great way to keep you focused, motivated and positive. We all need high energy levels in sales, and what we see around us can often affect our mood and mindset.

Many sales environments might already have motivational pictures and messages on the walls. However, you can create your own personal visual motivations.

Family photos are often a good place to start, seeing your loved ones will provide confidence, spur you on and pick you up when you're down. Other great visual aids are the things you want, expect and dream of. Your next house, your dream car or a future holiday you've got planned. You're looking for different things that can make you feel happy, excited, driven and motivated. You need to visualise yourself with the things you most desire, as thoughts really do become things. I discuss visual motivation in more detail in chapter 9.

Tell yourself that the next successful call, booked meeting or closed deal is getting you one step closer to the things you want and expect.

We all require a little inspiration sometimes; this is a good time for the next section...

39. INSPIRATION

Inspiration is a key ingredient in sales and can help drive you towards success.

Inspiration can be found in many forms, it can be a person, or people, a story, a song, a picture, a memory, there are so many.

You can have many sources of inspiration, and pick and choose the ones you think or know will help you at any given time or on any given day. If you can draw on your source of inspiration when required and if it can drive you, push you and inspire you to greater success then continue to be inspired. In chapter 9 I discuss these subjects in greater detail. **(Q) Who and what inspires you?**

40. DEAL IN PRINCIPLE. 'DIP'

This is one I'm rather proud of, as I created the concept, adopt the technique and continue to champion the merits of this to others in sales.

In essence, the DIP technique is simply asking your prospects & customers to commit to a successful outcome if you achieve what's required, before you've even quoted them. It's like saying 'if I do this, that and the other have we got a deal?'.

Although you'll word it much better than this of course using the information you'll acquire, and rather than saying 'have we got a deal', you'll initially say 'will I be in a position to agree a deal with you?', I'll explain why in **Chapter 4. CLOSING: If you're not closing then you aren't selling**

The 'this, that and the other' are down to you and your prospects & customers to determine and agree. Your prospects & customers will be giving you an outline of their requirements as part of the quoting process. You will use this information to create your DIP.

When you've understood this technique, adopted it and benefited from it, you really will appreciate the importance of it.

41. WHEN YOU OPEN AND CLOSE THE BOOK IN A MEETING

If you attend meetings with your prospects & customers then it's important to understand, appreciate and implement this technique.

Now, I say 'book' in the headline for this technique. What I mean by this, is when to start talking business and when to stop, it doesn't literally have to mean book. It's just that often you'll have a folder, notebook or laptop with you that accompanies you when you're speaking to your prospects.

The conversations you have with your prospects & customers before and after your meetings start are really important in terms of building rapport. They will also have strategic significance too.

Those all-important chats whilst you're ordering drinks and settling in can make the difference between a productive and positive meeting and a flat, negative meeting.

Those all-important chats whilst you're packing your things up and getting ready to leave are essential too. You can use the positivity and energy of your (informal) wrap up chit-chat, to catch your prospect and/or customer off guard and encourage them to give you extra snippets of information. You'll often find this is when you acquire your deal in principle (DIP) too.

I will explain this technique in greater detail, in the field sales section of **Chapter 8. SALES ROLES**

42. ALWAYS BE CLOSING

If you aren't closing, then you aren't selling!

In **Chapter 4. CLOSING** I discuss all things 'closing' and look at the various closing techniques available.

Closing is an art form and the most important ingredient in your sales armoury. There is no point working your socks off and acquiring opportunities from new prospects if once you've quoted you can't close the deal.

A close isn't a magic wand at the end of the sales process, it's built, shaped and delivered. Your close starts from the moment you first speak to your prospect and/or customer, your close builds throughout your interactions, using your powers of persuasion and the belief you 'can and will'. Your close ends with a yes and an agreement to buy your products & services.

Although there are many closing techniques, the best close is always the one that gets the YES! Remember the A, B, C of sales and Always Be Closing!

43. SET GOOD EXPECTATIONS

Setting good expectations is very important.

If your prospects & customers continually know what to expect, and you deliver upon those expectations, you'll often be rewarded for it. For instance, when you're quoting a prospect let them know what you'll be doing, how you'll be doing it and when you'll do it by.

When you're lead generating, let your prospects know what's required and what the steps are towards you being in a position to be able to quote them.

Remember, when you set clear expectations, you'll often find your prospects will reciprocate. You'll be in a much better position to find out when they'll call you back, when they'll provide you the information you require, what their quoting process is and when they expect to make a decision.

In sales the best way to avoid insecurity or frustration is to simply set good expectations with your prospects & customers, on what you'll both be doing. There is nothing worse than waiting for a call back and it not happening or waiting on information that isn't sent or waiting for a decision that doesn't arrive. All this can be avoided by ensuring that from the get-go you and your prospects & customers have a mutual understanding that the expectations you both set will be delivered.

Setting good expectations and delivering upon them says a lot about you too. You do what you say you'll do, and that's important when building rapport and gaining trust.

44. STOP THINKING ABOUT YOUR COMMISSION UNTIL YOU'VE CLOSED THE DEAL

You're in sales, you have a commission structure, great. You know what your basic wage is, and you know what your targets are, perfect.

You should know what's likely, what's unlikely and what's possible if you put the time and effort in, in terms of performance and monetary expectation. You can play around with these scenarios as much as you like, and I encourage you to dream, plan and motivate yourself. However, the reality is that you'll only earn commission from closed deals and often by hitting your targets.

Now is the time to get down and 'do' and stop thinking about commissions and bonuses until you've closed your deals and got them over the line. When you become so motivated by money that it's all you think about, or worse you spend money before you've earned it, you'll only ever head one way, and that's to disappointment and failure. You've got to get the balance right.

Your prospects & customers will be aware you'll be earning a commission and they certainly wouldn't begrudge that. However, they expect you to earn your coin and expect you to ensure that your motivation is to provide them the best deal and service possible. They don't want your commission to determine what products & services you quote them and what leads your agenda. As you've read in this chapter **26. IT'S NOT ABOUT YOU IT'S ABOUT THEM**

94

Your 'why sales?' is likely dominated by money, great, I'm with you. However, get the balance right, and ensure that you don't get too far ahead of yourself, it won't help you, it will distract you and it will be evident in your approach.

If your commission structure and targets are fair, then do your job, close your deals and earn your coin. Just don't get ahead of yourself, keep your eyes on the prize and "take care of the pennies and the pounds will take care of themselves". In this case, the pennies are your closed sales and your pounds are the commissions you'll earn.

45. CUSTOMER TESTIMONIALS

Customer testimonials are ESSENTIAL, so much so I've had to write this word in capital letters!

Customer testimonials are so valuable when it comes to providing reassurance and confidence in you, your company and your products & services. You should obtain as many customer testimonials as you can and have them feature on your website, marketing material and even within your proposals!

Sometimes, it's good to obtain a customer testimonial in the same location as your prospect, or the same industry, or of a similar company size and stature. Of course, you won't necessarily already have testimonials from many of your existing customers, but you can contact them as and when required. Some existing customers will be happy to provide first-hand testimony via a phone call or email directly to your prospects. Encourage this, it makes a huge difference to getting your deals over the line.

Also, when using customer testimonials, it's a good opportunity to name drop. You should name drop as much as possible, why wouldn't you crow about the businesses (and people) you supply, especially if they are known by your prospects. I discuss name dropping in this chapter **47. NAME DROP**

A testimonial is essentially a written 'static' recommendation to others. So, consider taking this a little further and request 'live' recommendations from your customers.

46. RECOMMENDATIONS FROM YOUR CUSTOMERS

The best way to achieve successful longevity and consistency in sales is to ensure that you've got other people championing you and recommending you, your business and your products & services to others. I also discuss this within this chapter **48. IT'S NOT WHAT YOU KNOW IT'S WHO YOU KNOW** and **51. FRIENDS, FAMILY AND COLLEAGUES**

There's no better recommendation than from your customers. Some of your customers will recommend you naturally. However, it's likely they didn't go out of their way for you. You, your business or your products & services probably cropped up in conversation. This is a good sign; it means you're an attractive proposition to others and worth recommending.

If a trusted customer can vouch for you, your business and your products & services you're already halfway there.

Now you know this, you need to understand that it's your job to encourage and ensure your prospects & customers are recommending you more often. Prompt them to do so and include this in your deal in principle (DIP).

For those new to sales or for those that don't receive many recommended sales, you'll need to invest in this approach and understand that the first few people you sell to, you might be on your own! Plant the seed early to your prospects that if successful you're looking to build and grow this trusted network of customers.

Your prospects will appreciate, respect and share your intentions and when the prospects become customers it won't be a surprise when you then ask for recommendations.

Remember, the person that recommends someone else to you will also be viewed favourably if you do a great job. It's a win-win!

When you sell to a new customer that's originated from a recommendation, it's an even easier conversation to ask them to continue this trend for you. That's how you found them so ask them to help you find others, just like them!

I bet you recommend people to others if you've received a great deal or service. Especially, if it then reflects well on you when you've put a smile on someone else's face. Great service and a good deal are infectious.

Invest in those first few apples, replant the seeds and you'll soon have an orchard of recommended sales to provide you the financial sustenance your life in sales requires.

47. NAME DROP

Name drop whenever and wherever you can!

The key to a good name drop is the impact it has on your prospects, and the difference it makes. The name you're dropping might be a person or it might be a company. It doesn't matter as long as your prospects are aware of the name.

You might supply a company that is known nationally, or locally, or within their industry. Or, you might have a contact who is connected in some way to your prospect and/or customer. The point is, you're sending out a message that you supply businesses and people they know, you're well connected, and you have a team of trusted allies that you (or they) can call upon to provide positive testimony.

The more touch points you can find to connect yourself to your prospects the better, as it'll further encourage and persuade them to use your products & services. As you build your customer base and trusted network of friends, contacts and allies, you'll soon find you'll be name dropping continually. It's what all the hard work was for!

The next section highlights and supports this.

48. IT'S NOT WHAT YOU KNOW IT'S WHO YOU KNOW

Now, let me be clear. Of course, you need to know your stuff. As you've already read in this chapter **1. KNOW YOUR PRODUCTS & SERVICES** and **2. KNOW YOUR FEATURES & BENEFITS**

However, much of what you sell might be to people you've never spoken to previously, or don't know that well. To be really successful in sales you need to have a large network of trusted allies and people that can provide positive testimony to you, your business and your products & services. To have a large support network is extremely advantageous especially if they know your prospects & customers, or, they work in the same industry.

Of course, the more connected and influential these people are the better, as they can open many more doors for you.

These trusted allies will also soon attract business to you and point people in your direction. Why? because you've asked them to and because they'll want to. Every customer you acquire can become a wonderful source of new business elsewhere if you consider the people and the businesses they also know.

You need to influence everyone you meet; everyone you speak to and anyone you can influence that is part of your social media groups.

Let people know what you do and why you do it, and don't ever be afraid to ask for help in acquiring new business. If you're as good as you tell people you are and your products & services can help make a positive difference to your customers then anyone that recommends you to others will also benefit from the praise and satisfaction that will come from a successful outcome.

You need to spend time recommending others, again, only if you're confident the people you're recommending will provide a great service. This will encourage the people you're recommending to do the same for you. However, you need to ensure you make this point to them, don't assume they will recommend you.

There's nothing wrong with securing a deal on the back of a 'recommend a friend' from someone you know. There is no extra prize or dent in pride for winning a deal because you've had a leg up.

You need to have a network of trusted allies that will recommend you, support you, champion you and vouch for you.

(Q) How many opportunities are you receiving from your network of trusted allies?

49. PERCEPTION

(Q's) How is your company perceived by others? and how are you perceived by your prospects?

Now of course, perception is in the eye of the beholder.

But if this is your prospect, and they have a negative opinion of you, your business or your products & services you might not get the chance to change their perception and even if you do, wouldn't you rather be talking about more positive things?

A prospect might not have any pre-conceived opinions about you or your business but trust me they'll be judging you from the get-go.

Have you ever considered your prospects might research you personally? They might look at Facebook, Twitter, Instagram and LinkedIn etc? *(Q) What does your social media profile and content say about you?*

You must ensure your social media supports you and doesn't work against you. In the next section **50. USE YOUR PERSONAL SOCIAL MEDIA FOR BUSINESS** I discuss this further. I've seen salespeople that might have a professional and well-rounded profile on LinkedIn but on Instagram, Twitter and Facebook they portray themselves as anything other. I'll also discuss social media in **Chapter 7. RESEARCH AND STRATEGY**

Look at your company website and view it with the same eyes as your prospects & customers. Ask questions of your marketing and IT team and give opinions if you feel it's justified, let's remember you want your website to support you in selling your products & services and provide confidence and reassurance in your business.

Positive perception is a valuable commodity in sales!

50. USE YOUR PERSONAL SOCIAL MEDIA FOR BUSINESS

As I discuss in **Chapter 7. RESEARCH AND STRATEGY** social media is a valuable research tool for you and your prospects. Social media also provides a wonderful opportunity for you to let your prospects & customers know more about you, you can interact with them on a personal level with a view to building an even greater rapport.

Your interactions might start with a simple retweet, a share, comment or like. You can start subtly and slowly with the hope your prospects then engage with you and learn more about you. If you've already done enough (at work) for your prospects & customers to know more about you, then your interactions via social media will have a greater impact, if you get your strategy right.

The point is, if your personal social media profile reflects you, in terms of showing you in your best light then you will almost certainly benefit when you interact with them back within your/their working environment. Remember, people buy from people.

As I also mentioned previously in **49. PERCEPTION** how you're perceived is important too. If your social media, is anything other than showing you in a good light, then obviously do not interact on those platforms. However, consider that your prospects might still be doing their own research on you. Look at your social media through the eyes of your prospects & customers, what does it say about you?

(Q) Is it time for you to give your social media a bit of housekeeping?

51. FRIENDS, FAMILY AND COLLEAGUES

Following on from **48. IT'S NOT WHAT YOU KNOW IT'S WHO YOU KNOW**, there is so much business that can come from friends, family and colleagues. If you ask them to help you find new business, they will, and often.

You'll receive new business from time to time organically from them, as they'll mention you, your company and your products & services in passing, if you crop up in conversation.

Many of your friends and family work for employers that can buy your products & services, or, they have customers, friends and colleagues that do. Your friends and family might not currently appreciate this, but by getting them to promote you, your company and your products & services is such a valuable resource for you.

You could even create an incentive for people to recommend you. Tell your family and friends that you'll provide them with a reward for helping you. When choosing your reward, ensure that it's appropriate and sufficient. Also, ensure that you pay up and deliver on your promise to them.

Ask your employer if they'd fund the incentive. Why wouldn't they? if it's attracting new business into your business without any marketing spend. Trial an incentive, get it working, and make sure it's successful. You'll then be in a stronger position to roll it out onto a larger scale with the support of your employer.

Write down the names of 6 people you know outside of your company (3 friends and 3 family members is a good start), the first 6 names that come to mind is fine.

Now, write down where they work and what they do. If you don't know what they do or where they work, then enough said! ...why not? ...go find out!

What opportunities are there in their company to buy your products & services?

What opportunities are there for their customers to buy your products & services?

If you do know what they do and where they work, have you ever asked them to help you find new business? Again, if not, why not? Don't wait or expect it'll just happen, make it happen.

Do they actually know what you do? Where you work? And what products & services you sell? If not, why not? You should be shouting from the roof tops to everyone about what you do, where you work and what you sell.

Opportunity is everywhere and it's always listening, so make some noise!

If they do know what you do, are they passing leads to you? If not, encourage them to help and support you, and again, if you need to, incentivise them!

Now, extend this list past 6, and continue for as long as you can. If you have a large family and lots of friends, you'll have a pretty substantial list to work with.

When it comes to work colleagues, this is also a wonderful opportunity that is often underused by salespeople. Think of your work colleagues that don't work in sales, do they recommend people to you? or pass leads to you? If not, why not?

You need to encourage all of your work colleagues to promote the products & services that your company provides. It's win-win, the more business being generated by your company can only be a good thing in terms of stability, prosperity and job security for all.

You can incentivise your work colleagues in the same way you reward your friends and family. Speak to your employer and ask them to support this, (if you're not already doing this) they'll wonder why they hadn't adopted an employee incentive scheme before.

If it's successful, you'll not only be rewarded with a share of new leads coming into your sales team, but you'll also receive a 'high five' from your boss for the idea.

In summary, your friends, family and colleagues are a valuable resource in lead generation. Don't assume or expect them to recommend you, you need to encourage them to do so. Educate them, excite them and if you need to, reward them.

The more people you have championing you and helping you find new opportunities the better. This is why it's important to build a great reputation and a network of trusted allies in the quest towards future success.

52. WORK WITH YOUR COLLEAGUES, NOT AGAINST THEM

I'm always amazed when I speak to a salesperson that doesn't know what their company marketing plan is. Do you?

You should be assisting your marketing team and they should be assisting you. Especially, if you're receiving leads and business on the back of this marketing activity. Sales and marketing should work together and share ideas. There is so much talent, knowledge and experience that can come together and create magic, if you encourage this interaction.

You might think the success of your business is directly linked to the sales that are acquired by you and the sales team you work with. However, the reality is that everyone within your business plays an important role and you should all be supporting each other. That starts with you and everyone else in sales. You can't do this without everyone being on board and pushing in the same direction. You're a team!

You might have mixed perceptions about marketing, IT, accounts or customer services and these teams might have mixed perceptions about sales too.

Some will be accurate, and some will be fair. Some will be positive, but some will be negative. The inaccurate and negative perceptions you might have, or others might have of you have been created by simply not communicating with one another.

As a business owner, I always encouraged and supported interactions between the various teams within my business. Of course, sometimes it wasn't pretty, and some frank exchanges took place. However, my business was always the better for ensuring that every individual in our company understood the value of one another and appreciated that we all needed to be pushing in the same direction.

You'll soon realise that all this wrapped up is a pretty powerful combination when you're pitching your business to your prospects. When you're talking to your prospects about how incredible your business is and how talented and loyal your colleagues are, you'll mean it and it will show.

Q) What more can you do for your colleagues?

53. AT THE START OF THE DAY

How you start your day is important and can often determine the kind of day you'll have. This follows on from **11. LEAVE IT AT THE DOOR**

As you'll soon read in **54. AT THE END OF THE DAY** how you choose to end your day can also determine how you start your day. However, even if yesterday was a wonderful day, without the right mindset you can still allow other factors to determine your mood and your day ahead.

You need to expect that life will often get in your way and things from time to time will happen that might want to affect your mood and affect your day. If you can overcome these mini blips in your day and remain calm, positive and optimistic you'll actually find they happen a lot less. You'll also learn to react better, by being better prepared practically and emotionally.

Look! the point here is that you are in control of your mood. Expect the unexpected. Do what you can practically to avoid any mini blips but when they arise in the future say "hey ho" and appreciate that life will get in your way sometimes, rise above it, put it into perspective and keep smiling, you've got a big day ahead, ...go get 'em!

(Q) Do you start your day in the right frame of mind?

54. AT THE END OF THE DAY

(Q) What 'ed' do you most feel at the end of each day? Elated, dejected or frustrated?

Maybe it's none if these?

As I said in **53. AT THE START OF THE DAY,** in sales it's really important to start the day being positive. However, this all starts with how you end your day. How you end your day will often determine how you start the next day.

The key to how to end your day to ensure you start the next day with a spring in your step is to ensure that you get the balance right. You need to ensure that you don't beat yourself up too much but also don't go home saying there was nothing more you could have done.

If you go home beating yourself up, you will only indulge negative thoughts that will soon create insecurity and self-doubt. You will take these negative emotions into your next day, you'll be likely to fail, and you'll do nothing other than confirm what you already think you know about yourself. It's a self-fulfilling prophecy.

However, if you go home blaming everyone else other than yourself, you'll never improve because you're not looking at the issues within yourself that's causing you to underperform or fail.

The best advice I can give you is to go home each day with an understanding and appreciation of things that went well and things that didn't. Then tell yourself, what you'll improve on tomorrow, what you'll work harder at, what you'll forget and what you'll do again because it worked so well today. If you're able to write these things down even better. All this needs to be wrapped up with an 'I can, and I will' attitude.

Continually remind yourself each day why you're doing this, you answered this earlier in **Chapter 1. WHY SALES?**

55. DURING THE DAY

Now, don't undo all that good work you might have achieved at the end of the day and at the start of the next day by then allowing yourself to have a bad day.

During the day, is where the action is, where the drama is, where the energy and emotion is.

Look, you know yourself that your day won't be full of 'yes's' and that you'll have hurdles and challenges to overcome. As you read within this chapter **19. THE NEXT 5 CALLS** and you'll read in the telesales & telemarketing sections of **Chapter 8. SALES ROLES**, it's your ability to appreciate and understand that each call will be different, each prospect will be different, and each opportunity will be different.

If you're in field sales you'll appreciate and understand the same thing, not every meeting will be the same. In reality each day will be different, whether it was a successful day or not. It's these differences that make sales fun, interesting and of course at times challenging.

Ensure that what doesn't change during the day is your mindset, your belief, your drive and your enthusiasm. Ensure this and you'll end each day and start each day with a positive mood and mindset that will carry you through the day itself.

Oh, and whilst we're on a 'during the day' theme, one of the best things you can do throughout the day is to drink plenty of water…hydration is so important to a healthy body and mind. If you're thirsty it's too late, so drink water and often.

56. 8 HOURS SLEEP

This could be added to any self-improvement book, a good night's sleep is so important. In my opinion, 8 hours sleep is ideal and should be your benchmark.

This is as important as anything else I've mentioned in this chapter.

With little or no sleep, you won't function and won't perform at your best. After a good night's sleep, you'll feel refreshed, you'll be more positive and the decisions you'll make will be much more decisive.

It's obvious I know, but sleep is our recharge button. We drain our internal batteries throughout the day, and we need to be recharged overnight.

Often the reason for poor sleep is things on your mind. It's not getting to sleep that often means no sleep. A good night's sleep requires good preparation, care and consideration.

Get yourself into a bedtime routine. Switch off your tech at least an hour before bedtime, I know it's difficult, but it becomes easier when you feel the benefits. Clear your mind and calm your breathing by taking deep breathes. Slow things down, you'll soon be back rushing around in the fast lane tomorrow.

Have a notepad and pen by your bed. If you have something on your mind or something you don't want to forget then write it down, it will then be there when you wake up. You don't need to think about this anymore, that's for tomorrow now. If you're worried you'll forget, you'll be reassured that your notes will be waiting for you when you wake up.

Get into the habit of writing a positive message for yourself before bedtime, it can start with a 'good morning' and lead to 'attack the day' or something from this book like 'be yourself' or 'I can, and I will'

It's nice to wake up to you telling yourself "go get 'em!".

57. SELF-IMPROVEMENT

You're reading this book, so you've already made the decision to improve yourself, good for you! "Never stop learning, because life never stops teaching".

Self-improvement (often called self-help) is a choice that can only be made by you. Take time to consider what areas of your life you'd like to improve upon and then move forwards in the pursuit of knowledge, understanding and appreciation of those areas.

The learning resources available in this modern 'on demand' age, are immense. It's your responsibility to source the help required, so carefully consider the information you're looking for when making your decisions.

Once you've made a decision on 'what' help you're looking for and you know 'where' to find it, take a little time to research 'who' is providing the information, so you can trust their advice, as wrapped around many of their facts will be plenty of their opinions.

I'm also the founder of a business called Sales Whizz®. At the time of publishing this book in 2020, Sales Whizz® is under construction and with the 'thoughts make things' concept I'm watching my ideas come to life. I'll be providing sales coaching, so I'm happy to expand on this book with you and tailor the coaching to you personally and/or your business.

Send me a connection invite on LinkedIn, and a personal message too.

The Sales Whizz® website will also provide useful online tools and information to further assist you in your sales career. www.saleswhizz.com

Depending on when you're reading this book, much of what I'm working on might now be a reality and will I'm sure be of interest and benefit to you, your colleagues and your business.

When it comes to self-improvement, I'd suggest that you try a mix of various learning methods and see which ones suit you. These include:

• Sales coaching.

• Reading books.

• Listening to audio books and podcasts.

• Using online resources.

• Watching online videos.

• Attending courses.

• Joining a mentorship program.

The best advice I can give you is to allocate some of your time each day to learning. Notice I didn't say, 'find time' or 'make time'. You don't need to make it or find it, it's already there! You're reading this book right now! Why now? it must be a convenient time for you. Did you allocate this time for yourself? or, was this just an opportune moment?

Change your routine to accommodate learning. Small amounts of learning at a time is fine as long as it's often. When you're not working (for many this will be of a weekend) you can spend more time learning. If you want to attend courses or lessons then of course you'll need to allocate time to do this, an evening each week for instance.

If you let your employer know you're spending your own time learning they'll be much more inclined to support you, especially during work time, if you're learning has a positive impact on you, your company and your sales results.

Q) Did you know that the most successful people read books regularly?

Successful people often prefer to be educated than entertained.

58 - 74. 'BE':

(Q's) How many of these BE's define you?

I'm expecting you to say 'yes' to many of the questions I ask in this section. However, consider if you can BE MORE of these things.

58. BE PERSUASIVE

Persuasion is one of my favourite words!

If any one word sums up sales for me it's this one. In sales it's our ability to persuade that sets us apart. It's getting the balance right, don't persuade enough and you won't sell, as I've said before the product doesn't sell itself, you do! Persuade too much and you'll sound desperate and scare your prospects away.

In sales, persuasion is the ability to convince, encourage and enthuse a prospect and/or customer to buy from you.

(Q) Are you persuasive?

59. BE POSITIVE

You must have a positive attitude to succeed in sales.

Sounds obvious I know, but salespeople that are underperforming lure themselves to a negative place where they say 'can't' more often than 'can' and they become pessimistic not optimistic.

Positivity is as good for you as it is your prospects & customers.

We must convey a positive message to our prospects & customers. You want them to have a positive feeling about you, your company and your products & services. When you're feeling positive, you'll smile and dial on the phone and rather than being hopeful you'll be expectant of a positive response. Your prospects & customers will often mirror your positive attitude and demeanour.

Being positive, helps with many of the 'BE's' in this section.

(Q) Do you have a positive attitude?

60. BE ENTHUSIASTIC

If you can't be bothered to sell your products & services, then why should your prospects & customers be bothered to buy?

Enthusiasm will get you a long way in sales, it'll give you and your prospects & customers the energy that will fuel your interactions. Enthusiasm is infectious.

(Q) Are you enthusiastic?

61. BE CONFIDENT

Confidence is so important in sales.

How do you expect others to believe in you if you don't believe in yourself?

Self-belief is the essence of confidence.

Self-belief is you knowing you can and expecting you will! when you say this, you're not being naive and you're not being arrogant, you're being confident in your own abilities.

(Q) How confident are you in your own abilities?

62. BE OPTIMISTIC

Your cup is half full, not half empty.

If you 'expect to be well received' you will be.

Optimism is the ability to be hopeful and confident about the future or the success of something. In sales, this is essential. Your optimism will soon become a self-fulfilling prophecy, say "I can, and I will" with conviction, belief and positivity and the universe will reward you.

(Q) Is your cup half full?

63. BE OPEN-MINDED

Being open-minded is a really important quality to have in sales.

Being open-minded is the ability to consider new ideas in an unprejudiced way. If you open your mind to new ideas and other ways of thinking, you'll learn much more about yourself and others. Being open-minded allows you to listen to two sides of an argument and be much more considered before making a decision.

Some of the most creative people are open minded.

(Q) How open-minded are you?

64. BE RESILIENT

Resilience is the capacity to recover quickly from difficulties.

You're going to get plenty of knocks in sales and you'll be tested continually, it's a combination of all the things we're discussing in this (BE) section, such as your mental strength, confidence, positivity and enthusiasm that will ensure you are resilient to difficulties because you're expecting them.

As Rocky Balboa said "It ain't how hard you can hit. It's how hard you can get hit and keep moving forward".

(Q) How resilient are you?

65. BE TENACIOUS

As Vince Lombardi said, "Winners never quit, and quitters never win".

Tenacity is that determined stubbornness that tells you to get up, push on and to never give up. Never lose this quality, it's essential in sales and in life.

(Q) How tenacious are you?

66. BE BRAVE

People don't often consider themselves as brave. It's normally a word bestowed to you by others.

Being brave in sales, is showing courage, taking risks, daring to be different, never giving up and overcoming adversity.

When you're on the phone, attending a meeting, networking or public speaking there is a level of bravery required. Of course, the level of bravery required is dependent on how confident & skilled you are (and many of the other BE's in this section).

Fortune really does favour the brave.

(Q) Can you be brave when required?

67. BE RELENTLESS

Being relentless in sales is a great quality to have.

It's that determination to succeed and refusal to give up that will often get you over the line and winning time and time again.

It's working as hard and smart as required to achieve successful outcomes.

It's embracing repetition and continually moving forwards keeping your eyes on the prize.

(Q) Are you relentless in sales?

68. BE HAPPY

It's obvious I know, but if you're not happy you'll struggle to succeed.

Happiness is a very personal emotion; one person's definition of happiness is different to another. Understand what makes YOU happy and work towards this. If you're not happy your prospects & customers will know, maybe even before you do. You might think you can fake it, but you can't.

You might be unhappy with certain things in your life, but with a clear direction, with positivity, confidence and all the other key ingredients being discussed in this (BE) section, you know you'll get to a happier place, if you're not already there.

If you're unhappy, it's important to address 'why' and take the appropriate action to change how you're feeling. This involves being honest and open with yourself and sharing your thoughts and feelings with others. You can't fake happiness, and why would you want to?

Wanting to be happy and taking action towards your future happiness is a relief in itself, you've taken control of your emotional health & well-being and you'll instantly feel a little better.

So be happy NOW in this moment, especially whilst doing sales, your prospects & customers don't need to know anything other than you're happy now, today. Could you be happier, maybe? But the point is you're not unhappy and you're working towards a happier place.

(Q) What's your definition of happiness?

69. BE HONEST

Honesty is the orchard of your integrity.

Integrity is the quality of being honest and having strong moral principles.

Honesty starts from within, being honest with yourself. When you're honest with yourself, you're much more likely to be honest with others.

(Q) Are you honest with yourself?

70. BE GRATEFUL

Being grateful and showing gratitude is important.

Being grateful is often followed by a thank you. 'Thank you' should be said much more in life, don't you agree?

We can be grateful for so much in life and it's important to share your gratitude with others. When doing this you'll also be sending out your grateful tones & vibrations to the universe! and the law of attraction will often reward you. Wanting more is great, essential in fact in sales. However, remember to be continually grateful for what you do have, not just the material things but more importantly, family, friends and good health.

(Q) What are you most grateful for?

71. BE YOURSELF

Being yourself is important on so many levels.

It's easier to be yourself than to act out a persona that's not yours.

It's a difficult act to live up to when you're not being yourself, as you'll need to maintain the personality of the persona you're acting out.

When you're being yourself, you'll connect with many more prospects & customers as they'll see you, for you. When you're being yourself, you'll share your own opinions and you won't be afraid of critique or failure.

It's easy being yourself, it's you, no one knows you better than you do, and no one can be you, better than you!

Like yourself and be yourself.

(Q) Are you being yourself in sales?

72. BE WHO YOU ASPIRE TO BE

Being who you aspire to be, still means being yourself, there's no getting away from that, and why would you want to. It simply means that you will learn, adapt, evolve and improve to become the person you want to be. It's still you at the very core of this, but that better upgraded version of yourself that you're aspiring to be.

To help, visualise where you'd like to be in 12 months and also in the next 3 to 5 years and work towards this starting now, today.

You can be this person now, of course you've got to go on the journey before you can get to the destination but that doesn't mean you can't make subtle changes now that will highlight your intentions to those around you and to the universe!

You'll think differently, be more confident, be more optimistic, be more determined, be more tenacious, you'll be more of the things I'm discussing within this (BE) section. By thinking about and 'being' the person you aspire to be, you'll arrive at your destination much sooner than the time you've set yourself.

Once you've made a 3 to 5 years plan, make a 10 years plan and so on. You need to set your own personal timeframes and you need to be setting your own personal goals too. The point is, it's good for you to make your intentions known to yourself and to the universe!

Of course, your plans, dreams and goals can and will change, but the point is you're working towards something better than today for a brighter tomorrow and beyond.

(Q) Who do you aspire to be?

73. BE LIKED

In this modern age of social media, people have a fascination and desperation around being liked. People will express an opinion online that they don't even agree with and would not share in person, just to be liked.

Well, in sales, being liked goes a long way too. ***However***, be liked for being you, being honest and genuinely being able to back up what you say. Being liked just so you can get your foot in the door isn't enough, being liked just to get your deal over the line is a false economy and you'll be working your socks off climbing apple trees never to benefit from a growing orchard, where you'll pick low hanging fruit from time to time just because you're genuinely liked.

(Q) Are you liked by your prospects & customers?

I know some of these questions are tough to answer, but with this one in particular you genuinely might not know. The point here is to understand and appreciate that being liked, comes back to being yourself. If you're being open, honest and genuine with a sprinkle of confidence and drive you'll be liked by most people you meet. They'll be rooting for you too and will want you to do well. Your prospects & customers will tell others they like you, they really will.

Be liked for being a good person and for doing your job to the best of your abilities. Go that extra mile and put a smile on the face of everyone you meet, they will like you for it and more importantly you'll like yourself.

74. BE THE OPPORTUNIST

Opportunities will arise often; you need to be aware of them and seize them. *(Q) Are you ready to react to opportune moments?*

There will be opportune moments to engage with your prospects & customers where you'll find them much more receptive, you just need to keep your eyes and ears open for them. There will be opportune moments to acquire new prospects and receive quick wins, if your opportunistic radar is switched on.

Being an opportunist, is about having the ability to react quickly when opportunities arise. It's about not having tunnel vision but having a peripheral vision for the things around you.

There will be opportune moments when you're interacting with your prospects & customers where the conversation can change based on something you've seen, heard or know.

75. HIGH FIVE AND WHOOP

(Q) When is the last time you gave or received a high five

Sales requires high energy, positivity and a desire to win.

Sales can and should be FUN! When we win, it's important to acknowledge this to yourself, to your colleagues and to the universe!

A high five is a worldwide symbol of good. It has a universal language and a universal message.

You can give them and receive them. They are inclusive and require another person to participate.

You will always associate a hive five with good intentions. Likely, it was after you or they had done something well.

Or, after you or they had achieved something.

Or, to energise you or someone with the hope of providing reassurance, confidence, strength or support.

Or, to say thank you.

Or, to greet someone

Or, to say farewell.

I encourage you to high five and whoop, ... yes whoop! often.

Chapter 3. WORDS, TIMING AND TONE:
What you say, when you say, how you say

Words, timing and tone are the key to your sales pitch.

Before we get technical, let's keep it simple.

Whether you're on the phone or face to face it's essential to know 'what' you'll say, it's key to know 'when' to say it and oh so important to know 'how' to say it.

Let me be clear, a salesperson is only as good as their sales pitch.

There are also two types of sales pitch when you're lead generating and prospecting for business. I like to call them the 'initial' sales pitch and the 'actual' sales pitch.

By splitting your sales pitch into an initial pitch and an actual pitch you'll understand and appreciate the differences between the two approaches and combine them effectively to close your deals.

In **Chapter 4. CLOSING** I'll discuss how the close actually starts from the very first contact you have with your prospects & customers. Every interaction (call, meeting, email etc) you have with your prospects & customers can take you one step closer to a closed deal.

Your prospects will be judging you from the get-go and considering you, your business and your products & services throughout. So, even though the initial sales pitch is pre-quote and the actual sales pitch is when you quote/have quoted, both sales pitches combine, support and complement each other when you're closing your deals.

The initial sales pitch gets you to the stage where you'll be invited to quote the prospect, you understand their requirements and you have a good idea of what's required to close the deal.

In **Chapter 2. SALES FUNDAMENTALS** I discussed the deal in principle (DIP). It's at the end of the initial sales pitch that you'll want to have the DIP agreed ready for your actual sales pitch.

Of course, you might work in an environment where the prospect comes to you and requests that you quote your products & services to them. If so, great, you'll advance to the actual sales pitch much sooner.

However, part of the initial sales pitch is building rapport and trust. It's also about providing reassurance and an understanding of the prospect's requirements. So, there's still much to learn from understanding and perfecting both the initial sales pitch and the actual sales pitch.

Ok, let's look at both sales pitches in more depth:

The 'initial' sales pitch

Where you're effectively courting the prospect. Your fact finding, establishing a need and/or requirement and wanting to quote your products & services to the prospect.

Your initial sales pitch will often also involve speaking to 'the head of first impressions', if you're working within a telesales or telemarketing environment. You'll commonly know this person as the receptionist or the gatekeeper. I don't like the negative connotation of a gatekeeper, that's why in chapter 2 I discussed the best way to approach the head of first impressions and provide a new appreciation for the importance of maximising each and every time you call your prospects.

Your initial sales pitch needs to be constantly building towards the end game, it's about getting the balance right. Move too quickly and you can lose your opportunity, move too slowly and you'll lose the prospects attention and appetite to buy.

Your initial sales pitch is the building blocks towards getting to the actual sales pitch. You'll only be in a position to quote your prospects your products & services once you've been invited to quote and once you've established their requirements.

The end game might take multiple calls and meetings or might take a couple of calls and no meetings. Ultimately, the time it'll take to close a deal will depend on the products & services you're selling, the prospects appetite to buy and your ability to persuade and get your deal over the line.

You need to value, utilise and maximise each opportunity with your prospects. Even a short phone call can provide valuable information.

In chapter 2, I talked about how to record all kinds of information and use it to your advantage. You'll use the information you've collated to start future conversations with your prospects, you'll use it to shoe horn information into your discussions and you'll use it to build rapport and to gain trust as it'll show you've been listening, and on occasions you'll even use it against them.

Your ability to record information and utilise it, is essential within your initial sales pitch. Each call to the prospect can provide more key information and provide an opportunity to use the information in your pursuit of meeting your sales objectives.

You should know what your mini objectives are along the way, they're like stepping stones on your sales journey to destination 'closed deal', be that by booking an appointment or being invited to quote for the prospects business.

If you know that you're more likely to close your deals by first meeting your prospects, then focus on this as your first objective in terms of the initial sales pitch.

If you're in telemarketing and your initial sales pitch only takes you as far as booking an appointment for a field sales person or as far as being invited to quote by your prospects (for someone else to then quote) then it's even more imperative that you get the initial sales pitch right before handing the prospect over to someone else. Especially if you're then paid a commission on the back of a closed deal.

In chapter 2, you'll have read many of the tips and techniques I shared in regard to your initial sales pitch. Now is the time to create your sales pitch and wrap these tips and techniques around it.

The 'actual' sales pitch

Where you've ascertained the prospects requirements and you've been invited to quote your products & services to them. Ultimately, it's this actual sales pitch that will lead you to a yes or no, a closed deal or a lost deal.

Don't think for one minute the hard part has been done in your initial pitch, far from it. Now isn't the time to take your eyes off the prize, sure high five and whoop for getting this far, however, you've now got to close your deal.

Some prospects & customers will have to obtain a few quotes and you might simply be one of their quota?

The prospect might already have made their decision and will be staying with their current supplier and you're only involved to make the current supplier match your price?

If the prospect is a corporate customer, then you might simply be one of the selected few that can tender for their business?

Whether this is the case or not, you've got the opportunity to quote which means you've always got a chance to win the deal, if you're persuasive enough and your deal matches or exceeds their requirements. As you get more experienced, you'll get better at working out which prospects might fall into these categories, however, I've never really cared one way or the other.

In the early months of my sales career I closed deals where to someone on the outside they'd assume I'd receive a no, and lost deals I thought were a certainty. I quickly took the stance that I'll assume nothing other than I've got the opportunity to quote and I'll win if I'm persuasive, tenacious and relentless enough, even if the odds are against me. I knew I wouldn't close all deals, that's unrealistic but at the same time I was confident I'd close what was required to move me forward, hit my targets and earn me plenty of commission.

As I got more experienced and even more confident on the phone and within meetings, I'd broach (within conversations with my prospects) the subject of prospects that would stay with their current suppliers for far too long and didn't have any intention of moving suppliers. Of course, I wouldn't be talking about the prospect I was directly talking too (wink wink), I'm generally talking about others I might have come across. However, what I knew was that I was putting myself onto a more even playing field with all my prospects, especially those that recognised themselves within my description.

My deal in principle set out what I needed to do to win their business. I knew that if I ticked those DIP boxes, they would find it very hard to say no without being reminded and challenged, which I've done regularly where I've received a no, and then turned it into a yes. It's a skill in itself, and something I discussed in chapter 2.

I'd like you to look at your sales pitch in a different way, let me set the scene:

Let's imagine you're playing a friendly game of baseball in your back garden with a child and you want to make it easy for them. You're the pitcher and they are the batter. Your objective is to help them hit the ball and achieve a home run, when this happens, you'll both be happy. So of course, very different to a real baseball game where you're trying to prevent the batter from hitting the ball.

You're now conscious that if you throw the ball too quickly or you make it too difficult, they'll more than likely miss, and you won't see them achieve a home run.

Ok, let's elaborate on this a little further and look at it from a sales perspective, we'll introduce the catcher into this too. The catcher is the person who stands behind the batter with the big glove!

You're the 'pitcher' (the salesperson).

Your prospect is now the 'batter'.

The 'catcher' is the dead tone of a telephone.

A good sales pitch is like a slow, soft pitch in baseball. The more able the batter (your prospect) is to hitting the ball (understanding and liking your sales pitch) the more likely you are to move to and then past first base with them (the sales process) and ultimately you'll close a sale and both achieve a home run together!

When you watch an actual game of baseball, you see the catcher behind the batter waving codes and messages to the pitcher, the pitcher then conceals what they're about to do and throws their pitch to the catcher with the sole intention of not allowing the batter to connect with the ball. A bad sales pitch is just like this, you'll confuse the batter (your prospect) and end up pitching your ball (your sales pitch) to the catcher (the dead tone of a telephone). Your call & sales pitch is over.

The foundations of all sales are built on being able to say the right words at the right time in the right way, we must get the prospects & customers attention, we need them to listen, we need them to interact with us and we must get them on our side.

WORDS - What you say

Your words are essential, and you must choose them wisely.

Your choice of words will need to provide detail, clarity and an understanding of your subject matter.

Your choice of words can allow your positive tone to flourish.

Your choice of words and the ordering of them are essential if you want your conversation to flow and move towards a successful outcome.

You must use positive words and avoid negative ones.

The words you choose must also have positive connotations. As an example, would you say contract or agreement? Essentially, they are the same thing, but don't you think agreement sounds much nicer? more collaborative, more like you've shook hands on a good deal based on trust. Contract sounds like it's tying them in to something that they can't get out of, it's like it's all about them signing on the dotted line and nothing more. In my experience, agreement wins every time.

Positive words and positive speak are so important in sales. I'd suggest that to ensure you're using positive language at work; you also use the same positive language at home and socially. We must become the people we aspire to be, positive speak really is infectious, it will encourage people around you to also speak more positively.

When constructing your sales pitch and your approach in terms of the words, sentences and questions you'll use be mindful that it's your choice, you're in control of your vocabulary. Choose words that best promote you, your business and your products & services.

Choose questions that are both open and closed and use them to adapt to the person you're speaking to and to the conversation itself. Open questions are obviously likely to receive a longer answer than closed questions. The answers to these questions can provide useful fact-finding information and can often encourage and lead onto your next question. Open questions are also ideal for getting your prospects & customers to speak, especially if they are either quiet or not engaged in the call. Open questions will allow your prospect an opportunity to think, reflect and provide their opinions.

Closed questions are likely to receive a shorter answer, often a yes or no. However, if your prospect chooses to elaborate on these closed questions and its useful info let them speak, you'll learn much more from listening.

It's your ability to use open and closed questions in your sales pitch that will ensure you keep control, acquire information, build rapport and move the conversation along.

Let me be really clear at this point, I'm not a fan of ever having a script in front of you when making a telephone call. You'll sound like a robot, you won't listen to the prospect and believe me, if you're going to be successful in sales, you'll follow the 70 / 30 rule. 70% listening and 30% talking. If you can lower your talking percentage and increase the listening percentage further into the call, even better.

You'll hear many people tell you to follow the 80/20 rule (80% speaking and 20% talking), for me, this is unrealistic on a regular basis. If you ask the right questions and speak at the right time allowing the call to flow and move forwards, 70 / 30 is just fine and has worked perfectly well for me and my sales teams over many years.

Getting a prospect talking is essential, especially if it's providing you good information and moving the call forwards towards a positive outcome. A script simply won't allow you to react and adapt within the call and it won't allow your personality to shine through. You have

2 ears and 1 mouth for a reason, so learn to zip it as and when required.

My advice is to write out and act out a few mock calls. This'll get easier over time as you'll experience a whole lot of different scenarios, people and responses. You'll construct a two-way script knowing that it will never be used, all you'll use are pointers from it. It's the best preparation you can have.

I've had numerous mock conversations with myself over the years, playing the roles of both myself and the prospect in advance of a call or a meeting, so I could prepare for as many eventualities as I could. Practice really can make perfect. However, I've always found it fun going into a real call or meeting and having a curve ball thrown at me. Personally, I always think I'm best when I'm having to think on the spot and work a little harder and smarter.

The way I see it, if I've done my prep, done my research, believe in my products & services and expect to be well received I'm often likely to achieve what I set out for, which is a positive outcome. I can soon bring the call or meeting back to the structure I'd like, and so can you. A curve ball also provides you an even greater knowledge and experience, so you can react to a similar scenario you might face in the future.

Remember, your preparation needs to include and consider your tone and timing. The words you choose to use are essential to allow your tone to flourish. Your timing is so important to the positioning of your words within your sales pitch.

TIMING - When you say

It's great knowing the words you'll use within your sales pitch and it's reassuring you've got a good idea of what you'll say.

132

Timing is about when you say these words, ask those all important questions, decide at what points you interject, decide the length of your narrative, the length of your pauses and most importantly when you choose to lift the call and move it forwards to the next level with the intention of receiving a positive outcome.

Understanding and appreciating timing, in conjunction with your words and your tone will allow you to adopt and deliver the best possible sales pitch.

TONE - How you say

Your tone is just as important as the words you use, in fact I'll go one step further and say it's more important.

Of course, you must do yourself a huge favour and choose positive words and superlatives to allow your positive tone to flourish. However, sometimes the tone itself can help you choose your words.

Your words and your tone are a complex and beautiful partnership.

Your tone will encourage, support and amplify persuasion, enthusiasm, confidence and charm.

You're already better with your tone than you might realise, let's look at 2 real life situations where you'll often change your tone:

When talking to a baby you change your tone to suit the situation.

You might be softly spoken at first.

(The baby then smiles).

You become more energetic and excitable, maybe a little high pitched or a little silly.

(The baby then laughs).

You repeat certain words over again and thrive on the reaction you've created.

You know the baby doesn't understand your words so your tone in conjunction with your happy face leads the way.

When you're making a complaint, you'll change your tone to suit the situation.

Let's imagine this is the 3rd time you've made the same complaint to the company you're calling, so you're already a little annoyed.

The person you're now speaking to is new to you, so you give them the benefit of the doubt. Your tone might initially be calm, but there's an authority and frustration within your voice.

(The person you're speaking to isn't listening and isn't helping).

Your tone becomes a little louder and much more assertive and the words you're using have been chosen to perfectly match this tone.

(The person you're speaking to apologises and resolves the issue).

Your tone softens and you sound relieved and grateful your issue has been resolved.

Your tone changes continually throughout the day, depending on who you're speaking to. Take more notice of your tone and understand and appreciate it better.

Your words, timing and tone are the essential ingredients to a great sales pitch. If you continue to evolve, appreciate and understand this, you'll have every chance of a long successful career in sales.

However, always appreciate that the only measure for success in sales are closed deals. If your sales pitch leads to a 'yes' and a closed deal, then your sales pitch was obviously a success. Look back at the journey that led to closing this deal and learn to repeat the words, timing and tone that was successful for you. Of course, each prospect is different and you'll adapt your sales pitch accordingly, however, you'll find that the vast majority of your successful sales pitches will have many similarities in terms of what you say, when you say and how you say.

If your sales pitch leads to a 'no' then you need to look back at what you said, when you said it and how you said it. This doesn't mean you'll change anything as you won't close every deal. However, it's the gap between yes's that will determine when you need to tweak or fundamentally change your sales pitch and or/ sales strategy.

In the next chapter, I'll discuss closing. If you're not closing, then you aren't selling, and if you aren't selling you won't be earning commission, hitting your targets and achieving your goals.

Closing is the 'why' to your sales pitch.

Chapter 4. CLOSING:
If you're not closing then you aren't selling

If you're not closing, then you aren't selling!

Your ability to close a deal is essential in sales, it's this skill (yes skill) that will determine your success both professionally and financially.

Sure, using your sales abilities for attracting new prospects and positioning yourself to quote them is a skill in itself. However, all of this is useless if you ultimately can't close deals.

Closed deals and fulfilled orders are important measures of success in sales, as are your ability to hit targets regularly and earn commission on a consistent basis. Of course, if you're looking to advance professionally in your sales career, you'll find the path to ever greater success is born out of your ability to close deals.

There are various stages you'll go through within sales when pitching and quoting a prospect, this will also depend on the products & services you sell. Sure, some products & services can be sold within the first phone call, others more often are sold after a period of research, follow up calls, emails and meetings.

You need to understand what you're selling and appreciate the stepping stones and minimum time it often takes to receive a successful outcome. It's about getting the balance right and knowing the likely times it'll take to get your deals over the line.

Don't be naive and expect too much too soon, as you'll end up disappointed often.

Don't be pessimistic and expect little, as you'll end up disappointed often.

The only way to ensure you're happy and winning often, is to get the balance right, work at the pace required and then expect to win, and often! You'll close plenty of deals because you knew what to expect and how to meet and achieve that expectation.

Let's start this section with the deal in principle (DIP). If your DIP is done correctly, this will be the best closing tool in your sales armoury.

As I mentioned in **Chapter 2. SALES FUNDAMENTALS,** this is one I'm rather proud of, as I created the concept, adopt the technique and continue to champion the merits of this to others in sales.

In essence, the DIP is simply asking your prospects & customers to commit to a successful outcome if you achieve what's required, before you've even quoted them.

It's like saying "if I do this, that and the other have we got a deal?", although you'll word it much better than this of course using the information you'll acquire, and rather than saying "have we got a deal?", you'll initially say "will I be in a position to agree a deal with you?"…why would they say no (at this stage).

The 'this, that and the other' are down to you and your prospects & customers to determine and agree. Your prospects & customers will be giving you an outline of their requirements as part of the quoting process. In terms of what's required to get a deal over the line, that's for your prospect to tell you. You'll usually have a fair idea of what you can offer way before you actually provide your proposal to your prospects.

This is the time where you need to get that all important DIP. It doesn't seem much at the time, simply asking your prospect to say 'yes' to your future plans and intentions but believe me it's super powerful when you present your proposal.

The DIP's you'll agree with your prospects & customers will be along the lines of:

"If I can provide you what's required (then outlining their requirements back to them), surpass your expectations on service and ensure you receive a competitive price will I be in a position to agree a deal with you?"

Now, at the time the prospect or customer will often say yes or provide a positive response to encourage you to come back with a good deal as they don't really have a reason to say no, why would they? they want you to quote and it's obvious that you'd at least be in a 'position' to agree a deal with them.

You'll also ask for a decision date, a 'yes or no date'. This isn't always possible, but if you can get a firm decision date in the diary you can not only work towards this, but also remind your prospect of this date during the quoting process, and more importantly on the day itself. It will avoid the prospect procrastinating over their decision or giving you a whole load of excuses thereafter.

You'll more than likely receive a decision date window, rather than a day. Such as the end, start or middle of a month. However, even this might need to be encouraged and suggested to a prospect, as some might not have set themselves any timeframe or deadline in when they need or want to make a decision.

Quoting a prospect with no idea of when they'll make a decision often leads to a long drawn out quoting process and insecurity / frustration on your part.

Your prospects & customers will appreciate and respect the fact that by knowing the timeframes you're working towards will encourage and motivate you to provide a great deal. It also allows you to speak to suppliers and other people within your business (especially when forecasting) which again can ensure that your quote is based on possible fulfilment dates etc, which is important to all businesses.

It's always best if you can present your proposal to your prospects & customers rather than sending it to them in advance, via email or post. When you send your proposal in advance of speaking to them, you won't be on hand to answer questions and to guide them through the journey of the quote. I say journey, as of course price won't be the first thing they'll see, and nor should it be. However, some prospects & customers will turn to the page that has the price and skip past everything else.

Of course, if your price is right then good for you, however, this still might not be enough to get your deal over the line. The ideal thing to do is to meet them face to face with your proposal in hand. Or, if this isn't possible arrange a 30 minutes phone call and send the proposal to them via email whilst on the call. I call this 'hear the ping', you want to ensure that the email is sent and received at the start of your call, not beforehand. Although, you might not actually hear the 'ping' of their incoming email, you get the gist.

The DIP becomes powerful when you reiterate this immediately before you present your quote. Bear in mind that most prospects & customers were not even aware they had even given you a DIP when you first received it. Of course, I appreciate that not all DIP's will be the same as it will depend on what products & services you're selling, and of course depends on whether you're speaking to the decision maker or not.

However, the below example gives you an idea of what I'm talking about, it's not a script and it's not set in stone, and of course it's not how all your conversations will go…. you'll get the gist.

Before you present your proposal to the decision maker, you'll reiterate your previous conversation, along the lines of:

"When we spoke 3 weeks ago, you said that if I provided you what was required, surpassed your expectations on service and ensured you received a competitive price, you'd be in a position to agree a new deal with me" (pause) "Well I'm pleased to confirm I've done what's required. I can provide…"

(You'll then outline again their requirements back to them).

"In terms of service..."

(You'll then outline the service levels and commitments included and also provide customer testimonials providing reassurances of your service levels).

"For just..."

(You'll then outline the costs and also reiterate if there are savings to be made).

"I can start the sales process today as outlined in my proposal and arrange delivery on..."

(You'll then provide a delivery date or timeframe).

If your prospect or customer doesn't commit there and then, you're then able to ask what's holding them back as your DIP was on the basis if you got your deal right, you'd have a deal.

So, break it down and ask what's holding them back.... have their requirements changed? Is it what you've quoted? is it service? is it price? or something else?

Once you've established what's holding them back, ensure you now tick off and reaffirm the other positive factors in terms of agreement, before discussing anything else. You need to ensure that the things they are happy with and agree with are put to one side (imagine positive ticks and smiles alongside them).

You can then focus on the thing (or things) preventing them from agreeing a new deal with you today. Ensure that you now get a new DIP before re-engaging. You need your prospect to agree that if you do specifically what's now required and get this last thing (or things) over the line, you've got a deal, as everything else has been agreed.

142

Of course, there will be occasions where you've already done as much as you could, and you don't have any more wriggle room. This now comes down to your ability to persuade and to reassure your prospect that you, your business and your proposition is the best.

You should also ask for recommendations within your DIP. If you ask, most (if not all) prospects will say they can recommend you to others IF you're successful. Again, to the prospect it doesn't mean much at this stage, it's just them saying all the right things to encourage you to get them a good deal. However, as soon as you've closed the deal you'll be asking & reminding them for their all-important recommended contacts, as per what they previously said they would do.

Start by asking for 3 contacts that they are happy for you to approach and ask them for an introduction to these people. This works even better if the customer you've just closed came via a recommendation. This is why, with each closed deal and each new customer you'll build a pipeline of new prospects and future customers.

You'll now need to understand and adopt a few other closing techniques to support your deal in principle as the DIP won't always be enough to get your deal over the line. Each has its own merits, and each is suited to a particular scenario you might find yourself in.

Your sales pitch and close will vary depending on your prospects. Each person you quote will have their own unique personality, their own agenda and their own motivation to buy.

There are so many different ways to close, here's a few to get you started.

Assumptive close

With this close you will intentionally assume that your prospect has already agreed to buy your products & services.

If delivered well, your prospect will go with you and continue the sales process. Of course, this works best with prospects that were intending to say 'yes' or were at least 50/50. However, you'll find from time to time that undecided prospects will also ride your assumptive wave.

The assumptive close will just speed up the process and will avoid you talking yourself out of a sale and giving your prospect more time to think and ask questions which might lead to a lost sale.

As an example of an assumptive close, you might say, "I can arrange delivery on Tuesday next week, does that day work for you?" You're assuming your prospect is happy to proceed which is why you're arranging delivery. You're not asking does the deal work for you, you're asking does this day for delivery work for you, if it does then you can assume the deal is on!

You will find from to time that the assumptive close will backfire on you or will evoke a response from your prospect along the lines of "who said I was ready to buy?" or "you're getting a little ahead of yourself". If this happens, you'll immediately play the naive card and ask what's holding them back from giving you the green light today. At least you're still talking about getting the deal closed now, today! and you'll know what more you need to do.

Alternative choice close

Following on from the assumptive close, you might decide to provide your prospect with a choice of two products or services. As an example, you might say "would you prefer that in red or blue?" Or "would you like to start with the silver or gold package?". You get the gist; you're assuming you've got the deal and are now fine tuning what's required by giving them a choice of two options. If they choose an option, then you'll know they've chosen you, your business and your deal!

Pro's and con's close

This close is used for prospects that are on the fence and at least 50/50 about whether to agree to a new deal with you.

You'll find that decision makers that procrastinate over a deal need a little shove (…or rather, gentle persuasion) in the right direction.

On a sheet of paper, outline with your prospect a list of pro's and con's. Write *pros* in the top left corner and *cons* in the top right corner with a line down the middle of the page. Encourage your prospect to tell you what THEY think are the pros of the deal, then the cons.

This in itself might be enough for them to convince themselves and say yes. However, if not, you can also fill in the blanks and add more pros, which they haven't included. You can then challenge, dispute or reassure them regarding their cons. Always ensure that the pros section has more advantages and is more attractive than the cons section.

Ask for the business close (direct close)

Yes, sometimes the best close is to simply ask for their business.

You've done your job well, quoted what's required and you're confident your quote will be successful. So, ask for the business "Are you happy to proceed?" or "Can we shake hands on this deal?"

You'll find your own style and the questions that best work for you.

The take-away close

This close is used when you're struggling to get a decision, or you feel that your prospect is procrastinating too much. It's very much a last-ditch effort to close a sale.

By taking the deal off the table you might find your prospect wants it more.

Most quotes will have an expiry date. My suggestion is that when you start the quoting process, base the deal you're offering on a month or a quarter (depending on the timescales involved with quoting your products & services). If you are then approaching this timeframe with no decision made, inform your prospect that you'll need to start work on revising the proposal on offer and reiterate that the current proposal will then be no longer available.

Reiterate that the revised deal you'll offer will still provide what's required and will still be attractive, it just might not be as good as what you'd originally offered. It's important that when you first quote your prospect, you're clear the deal you've negotiated for them is specifically based on the deal being closed (maybe even fulfilled) within a certain timeframe.

Also, don't suggest what your new proposal might look like. You need to tell your prospect that the new deal can't be prepared until the current deal expires. This then leaves your prospect with a decision to make, say yes now or take a chance on a worse deal. Make sure your prospects are aware that the new deal will definitely not be better than the current deal, your only hope is that you can offer the same deal again.

Fear of loss close

This close is similar to the take-away close.

We've all been faced with a salesperson saying, "this is the last one" or, "I've only got a few left and they're selling fast" and we've all took the bait and proceeded to order. Now of course, on occasions this is the reality and stock does sell out and deals end too.

It's the fear of loss that can sometimes get your prospects to make a quick decision.

If the fear of loss doesn't encourage a quick decision, then you know you've got plenty more work to do as your prospect isn't persuaded enough yet, so get selling!

Mini win close

Sometimes the best way to get your deal over the line is to let your prospect win. Let them feel like they've got something from the deal that wasn't originally on offer or wasn't originally included, it's a mini win for them (but still a big win for you!).

Some prospects will need to feel like they've negotiated hard and have done the best for their employer. If they feel they've pushed you further than what was originally on offer, or, have squeezed you to quote the best deal you possibly could, then encourage this.

To achieve this, you'll need to pre-plan, which is why it's a good idea to hold a few small things back to be used in the final stages of your sales pitch. Of course, it's getting the balance right, don't hold too much back as you still need your original proposal to be strong, competitive and attractive. Also, if you've said you'll quote your best deal first time, you'll then need to be ready to explain how you've pulled this extra rabbit out of the hat. That's easy, there's loads of reasons you can come up with for getting them what they wanted.

With experience, you'll soon start to get a feel for which prospects need a mini win.

You'll often use this close with the 'what would it take close?' below.

What would it take close?

With this close, you're hoping the prospect gives you a good idea of what you'll need to do to get your deal over the line.

If you've already quoted and the prospect is procrastinating then suggest you can speak to your boss to try and get some further squeeze, but before you do, you need to know from them "what it'll take, to get this deal over the line?". This close is often used with the mini win close too.

If the prospect was considering saying no to your deal, you might encourage the prospect to go way above and beyond what they expect to either scare you off or get an unbelievable deal which is way beyond what they actually expect.

If the prospect was 50/50 then you still might encourage them to do the same, however, you might actually find they provide you with a fair overview of what it will take to get your deal over the line.

Either way, if the prospect throws you a bone, then you're still in the running.

If the prospect is trying to scare you off then you'll know what they are expecting is way above what anyone on planet earth can offer and you can use this against them. Even though you know (that they know) what they are looking for is unrealistic, you can be naive and help educate them. You can then persuade, convince and prove to them that what you're offering is the best deal on offer.

If the prospect isn't looking for too much more, then give them the mini win if you're able to, and you feel without this you'll receive a no. However, before you give more you need to establish a new DIP. Ask your prospect or customer, if you get what they want over the line, have you got a deal? Even if you know you can, you must establish a yes to this question, without doing so, you risk offering them more and still waiting on a decision.

Try before you buy close

If you're selling the kind of products & services that allow your prospects to 'try before they buy' then use this to your advantage.

This technique is often called the 'puppy dog close' where you allow the customer to take the puppy dog home and return it after a few days if things don't work out. You're confident that the puppy won't be returned.

In summary, closing is what determines your success in sales. Each prospect is different and their motivations to buy will vary continually. If you understand, appreciate and adopt a fresh, varied and comprehensive closing strategy you'll be a in a great position to close plenty of deals.

There's plenty more closing techniques and hybrids of what I've already written within this chapter. The fun is creating your own, using your own style.

Chapter 5. OBJECTION HANDLING:
Use their excuses to your advantage

Objection (noun) an expression or feeling of disapproval or opposition; a reason for disagreeing.

Objection handling is an essential skill to have. I say skill, as like any skill it needs to be learned and practiced.

As I said in **ABOUT THIS BOOK**, if you're already working in sales, I could ask you to list a handful of regular objections you receive, and you'd happily list them. However, are you happy with the way you're reacting and responding to these objections?

Now, many of the objections you'll receive aren't actually objections, as defined above. Most of the time, they are simply reasons and/or excuses to not buy from you or not speak to you.

A common theme I'll discuss in this chapter, is using your prospects excuses against them. I see many of the excuses you'll receive as tactics adopted by your prospects to get you off the phone, prevent you from quoting them or to reject your proposal. However, what your prospects don't realise is that you can use their tactics against them and to your advantage.

As you'll read within this chapter, there's no set way to overcome an objection and no set rule either. You need to be inventive and creative and dare to be different. If you're prepared for the objections, excuses and tactics you'll receive you'll be best placed to counter them with your own tactics.

You must push back, don't hear 'no' and then give up immediately. You must be confident that you can and will overcome many of the objections & excuses you'll receive.

So, let's look at some of the common objections & excuses salespeople might receive, I've split them into two. The first section is pre-quoting and the second section is post-quoting. Essentially, there is a difference between the objections & excuses you might receive when courting your prospects and when you actually quote them.

I've also listed a few ways you can overcome these objections & excuses with some top tips too.

Of course, you'll receive many more objections & excuses than this and the way you'll overcome them will depend on you and your prospects. Each call and each prospect is different, and of course each salesperson is too! You'll find your own way and your own style. The best response is always the one that gets the best results.

PRE-QUOTING OBJECTIONS & EXCUSES

These are the objections & excuses you might receive when your lead generating and prospecting.

Most (if not all) prospects aren't wanting or able to tell you to 'get lost' either because they are nice people or they aren't brave enough, or a combination of the two.

In over 25 years of working in sales, I can't think of a single time any prospect has put the phone down on me. Sure, I've encountered rude prospects, that's part of the game. However, if you're polite, professional, fun and you 'dare to be different' you'll find most prospects are fairly responsive.

If a prospect hangs up on you, it says more about you than them. You'll have either been rude, outstayed your welcome beyond the point in which you should have accepted defeat, or you lied in order to get the prospect on the call.

There are some prospects who will find excuses or lie to you in order to get you off the phone. Of course, some prospects are telling the truth, if you assume that every unresponsive prospect is lying to you, it will have an adverse effect on your performance and mindset.

Go by the 50% rule. Assume that half the prospects that tell you they've 'just signed a deal', or 'it's not a good time to speak', or 'I'm in a meeting' etc are saying this just to get you off the phone. It's your job to try and figure out which prospects are telling the truth and which ones you need to chip away at more using your persuasive questioning skills. You'll make your own decisions on which prospects you'll re-approach in a different way at a different time.

As I said a moment ago, you'll often find that these aren't objections, they are excuses for not wanting to speak to you. It's your job to overcome these excuses, get the prospects engaged and buy yourself some time so you can build rapport and explain why you're calling with a view to progressing the opportunity.

To be a great seller you need to appreciate the role of the buyer. Some prospects are bombarded by salespeople, and they've tried the "I'm not interested" response but the salesperson kept coming back wanting to know why. They tried the "it's not a good time" or "I'm in a meeting" response but they know the salesperson will then call them back. So, in the end, some resort to lying and telling you things like "I've just signed a deal" in the hope that it will get rid of the salesperson without any push back and with the salesperson not feeling like they've failed. It also then buys them a longer period of time before they are called back.

I've just signed a deal

If you're regularly receiving this objection, then you really do need to look at your sales pitch. Why? ...well you can't be that unlucky.

Even the best salespeople don't call new prospects and find that they are regularly calling at the perfect time and the prospects are looking for a new deal, no one is that lucky. Sure, a few might have just signed a deal, but the odds will tell you that the majority are saying this to get you off the phone.

You'll need to gently interrogate the deal they 'say' they've just signed. I say 'gently' as to suggest they haven't signed a deal will lead to the dead tone of a telephone.

When was the 'just' a week ago, a month ago?

If the prospect thinks that you've accepted their excuse and are shortly to end the call, you'll actually find the call will last a little longer as the prospect will relax assuming the call is about to end.

So, if your initial response is "when are you next due a renewal?" or "when is the next opportunity to call you again?" …you get the gist; you're effectively saying that you're about to end the call with the knowledge of when you can approach them again in the future.

Dependent on what products & services you're selling will determine what the length of an agreement looks like so you'll have a fair idea of what the usual gap is between your prospects purchasing again, so ensure the timeframe you're given by your prospect is in line with what you know.

Now you've been given a future time to call again, you can use the… 'out of interest' approach. "Out of interest, …what did your new deal look like?", again, depending on what products & services you sell will allow you to ask this question being a little more specific and on point. The more specific your question the more likely you'll get a good response. The plan is to compare what they say they've ordered to what you could have offered, ensuring that what you could have offered was better.

If you've called the prospect before and you've previously acquired information, try and keep bringing it back to the products & services they used to have before they 'apparently' placed this new order. As you might find that these will be the products & services they still have.

The plan is to acquire as much info as you can as you'll approach this prospect again in the not too distant future. You might find at this time they are more responsive, or they provide a new excuse. They might provide the same excuse? Either way, you might choose to gently remind them they'd just signed a deal when you previously called.

However, you might find that whilst on the call the prospect is interested or asking buying questions, this will not only let you know that your instincts were right and they haven't just signed a deal but it will also allow you to progress the call and suggest that maybe the prospect could postpone or cancel their order if it's not been fulfilled.

On the next call you make to the prospect you might want to try a different approach. You know from your first call/approach that the prospect relaxes when they know the call is coming to an end, so rather than enquire about their products & services to then be told they've just signed a new deal or some other excuse, what you could do is simply tell them that sending you're sending them some important information regarding their products & services, and ask them to confirm the email address you have for them. If the prospect confirms that this is their email address (which they will because you knew this anyway), you can then say that you'll be in touch in a few days, when they've had a chance to look at what you've got to offer.

If the prospect says "that's fine" or provides some other form of acknowledgement or acceptance, it won't necessarily mean that's fine, it will often mean that the prospect wants the call to end. However, they didn't say they'd just signed a deal did they! so this excuse has been taken out of the mix for them. Now is the time to be remembered! as you want and need them to remember they haven't lied to you.

Before you leave the call, you'll be able to ask one or two more questions as the prospect is still relaxed because they know you're ending the call. Make these questions good ones with the hope that you further take away the 'I've just signed a deal' excuse and you get yourself in a position to be able to pitch the prospect on your next call/approach.

Top tip: If you're calling the prospect back within weeks of the original 'I've just signed a deal' call, as you suspect they haven't just signed a new deal, then it obviously pays to not be remembered on the original call. Unlike with most of your calls where you're looking to be remembered and will support this with emails and marketing material, your best option is to acquire as much fact-finding info (on the original call) as you can and then re-approach the prospect 'fresh'. The time to be remembered is when you're getting somewhere!

We're happy with our current supplier

Some prospects will say this whether they mean it or not, if they don't want to change suppliers and don't want to enact change. Some prospects will also say this to get you off the phone.

If your prospect is genuinely happy with their current supplier, then it's your job to understand the reasons why. It's also important to share their happiness and not instantly bad mouth the current supplier or tarnish their reputation. If you are too quick to dismiss their happiness and too eager to suggest you're better, you'll alienate yourself to your prospect. Much better to understand and appreciate why they are happy with a view to ensuring you naturally offer the same qualities and actually provide more.

Just because your prospect is happy with their current supplier doesn't mean they can't be happier. You'll often find its low expectations that have made the prospect happy, it's your job to raise expectations and highlight why your business operate at this higher expected level.

It's your job to outline what your qualities are and highlight what sets you, your company and your products & services apart from the competition. You haven't got long to do this, as you'll need to earn more time credits on the call. The first 30 seconds of a call comes for free, thereafter it's all about your ability to earn extra time credits and extend the call.

In **Chapter 7. RESEARCH AND STRATEGY: Knowledge with a plan of action** I'll explain that for many of your prospects you should already know who the current supplier is and know what their strengths and weaknesses are. I appreciate that for some, research can't be done for every prospect, however, the more research you do / acquire over time, the fewer calls you'll need to make and the more successes you'll have.

You must not bad mouth the competition to your prospect, as it's a sign of weakness on your part and it's unprofessional. However, what you can do is play the 'they're good but we're great' game.

Focus on your qualities rather than the current suppliers inadequacies. Find examples where although you're not being negative towards the current supplier, you're making their position weaker by promoting your strengths.

It's important to realise too, that for some there are other suppliers in the loop, especially if you're selling third party services.

For instance, if it was a mobile phone, there could be the company that supplied the mobile phone hardware and the network that provides the sim card and services.

If it was a car, there could be the company that supplied the car and the manufacturer that provides the servicing.

The prospect might be happy with one but not the other?

So, when they say they are happy, understand how many suppliers are in the loop providing the 'said' products & services and are they happy with them all. Appreciate the part that your company plays in this loop, and if you also provide products & services with the support of other suppliers then use this to your advantage, especially if the part you play is the part that they aren't currently happy with.

If you provide your products & services with no other suppliers in the loop, then good for you, you need to use this to your advantage within your sales pitch.

It's also important to understand when your prospect is able to purchase new products & services, as they might be in a contract. As they haven't given you this as an objection or excuse then it should indicate they aren't in any contract? however, you don't want to spend too long 'pitching' to find your prospect isn't in a position to do anything anyway.

Top tip: It's much easier to find out what your prospect doesn't like about their current supplier by first asking them what they do like. If you ask what they don't like first, you'll look like you've got an agenda and your prospect will shut down. However, it's only fair once you've ascertained what they do like to then ask, "what (if anything) would you change about your current supplier?" The hope is that your prospect provides you with some negative content about the current supplier that you can then use to strengthen your own position.

Send me more information

This is a common response, and a lazy one too. The prospect will let you think that they might be interested but they ask you to send them information for them to read before considering talking to you.

Many prospects will also use this excuse on the back of saying they are just about to go into a meeting or it's not a convenient time for them, so you then don't ask questions or start pitching them.

By saying "send information", some prospects are actually saying "go away" and "don't call back". They want you to assume that they'll call you if what you send them is of interest. The prospect thinks that they can kill two birds with one stone, they can end this call and end any future calls.

If you're asked to send more info there are a few things you can try.

You can go along with their request and ask them for their email address, the prospect will relax as they know you're about to end the call. However, before you go you'll need to know a little more about their current products & services in order to send the correct information. If your requests for this information are denied because the prospect says they haven't got the time, then use their own tactics against them. Thank them (using your most grateful tones) for allowing you the opportunity to send information, but tell them that rather than send a whole load of information some of which won't be of interest to them, you'd rather wait to speak to them again at a more convenient time to ensure what you're sending is more bespoke with the products & services they use and is of interest to them.

Suggest a time to call back to gather the info required so you can then send them the info required. By now, the prospect can't say "they've just signed a deal" and most will find it difficult to now say, "I'm not interested".

It's now your job to ensure that between this call and the next call you are remembered! You must do more research and start your next call on the back of the fact you're only calling back for more information 'as agreed', so you can send information to them. That way the prospect will again be relaxed that the call won't last long, although this time they'll need to 'throw you a bone' and give you more information. It's these stepping stones that might eventually get you to a position where you're pitching the prospect. Of course, you'll need to have the info ready to send and you'll need to follow up on this info, the plan is that by the time your prospect has received the information you've done enough to get your foot in the door.

You could say that your company doesn't send information, as it's costly and often unread. You could back this up by saying your company chooses to use its finances to ensure you have the best infrastructure, best customer service, best products & services and the best employees, which results in the best customers.

Sure, there is bespoke info you can send related to the specific requirements of your prospects but to send a whole load of info some of which would not be relevant to them seems wasteful and pointless. Again, use their excuse against them. As they've expressed an interest in more info, ask them what in particular would be of interest to them?

Also, let them know that you're pleased they are interested in more info as it indicates they are or will consider what you're offering.

Enquire as to why they'd like more info? is it good timing from you? are they currently in the market for your products & services? ...you get the gist.

Again, for many prospects this won't be the case, but hey ho, they led you down this 'send me more info' excuse, they'll now have to humour you and provide more info, Or, they can be upfront and admit they said this to get you off the phone which many now won't do.

You could say that you'll deliver the info directly, in person. Of course, if you're able to, if you're local or in the area.

If you're not in fields sales and the plan is for you to book appointments for others, you can still arrange for your colleagues to pop the info into them with a view to meeting them. I'm a huge advocate of maximising your time when you're out and about meeting prospects or customers. Whilst you're in the area / on route to and from your meetings it's important to try and meet new prospects with a view to moving things forward with them.

If you tell a prospect that you're in the area anyway, they won't assume you're making the journey just for them, this takes a little of the pressure away from them agreeing for you to 'pop your head around the door', as you're passing by that's all.

This is also a good chance to name drop, if the customer you are meeting is known to them locally.

When you start to benefit from this tactic, you'll then use it even though you aren't actually meeting anyone in the area. However, you can book multiple appointments in a row using the 'I'll just pop my head around the door' approach. So, when you said you was in the area, you now are. When you said you was meeting others, you now are.

Now, using this approach will also require you to once again use their excuses against them. When you respond to the 'send me some more information' request, you need to say something along the lines of "Great, I'm in your area a fair bit over the next few weeks, I'll pop my head around the door on Tuesday afternoon if that's ok? It'll give me the chance to meet you too". It's important you don't ask permission or ask when is a convenient time, as you'll only encourage another excuse. If they don't want you to hand deliver the info or don't want to meet you when you do, they'll soon tell you or tell you an excuse anyway.

You said you were in the area over the next few weeks (so you've took away any excuse of them not being able to find you a small window in that time), you've reaffirmed you're in the area and passing by (so there's no fear or pressure that your prospect will think you're making a special trip just for them) and you gave them a suggested day

162

without being too precise with time, if afternoon isn't suitable you can change it to morning, if they say that day isn't convenient you can throw out another day.

This tactic will also be used when looking to book meetings with prospects, not just for prospects that ask for more info.

Top tip: It's important that your CRM can assist you geographically as once you've got one prospect to agree to meeting you (albeit it briefly) whilst you hand deliver some information, you'll want to maximise your time in that area and meet others.

You'll need to then focus your activity to calling prospects in and around that area, or on route to and from their location.

Also, you can name drop a prospect as easily and effectively as a customer, even if you've never met the prospect. If you say you're going to see the 'name drop' on the same day you're seeing them that's fine, all true, if you then take information to them. If you've used a good name drop, one they'll know, one they'll be impressed by, then this could make a difference to how they perceive you and how responsive they become.

If you're asked what relationship you have with the name drop you'll reply with something along the lines of "the same as with you, I'm popping my head around the door with a view to working with them", …you get the gist, it's all true and you're being honest. Remember what I said in chapter 2, 'honesty is the orchard of your integrity'. However, of course, we can still play the game and bend the rules a little.

I'm busy / I'm just about to go into a meeting

If they were that busy, they wouldn't have answered or took the call. If they're just about to go into a meeting (or they are in a meeting), again, why are they taking calls? You'll often find it's as soon as they assumed you were 'selling' or understood what you were selling that they suddenly became too busy to speak or conveniently was on their way to a meeting.

As you'll read within **Chapter 8. SALES ROLES: Telesales & Telemarketing, Field Sales and Account Management** when you call a prospect, they are ALL thinking 'who are you and what do you want'. It's the natural position to take when you receive a call from someone you don't know. It's obviously your job to let them know who you are and more importantly why you're calling.

However, it's important to get the balance right, tell the prospect too soon why you're calling, and you might encourage the "I'm busy" or "I'm just going into a meeting" excuse. Take too long and you risk the prospect losing patience, asking you why you're calling and still giving you the same excuses as they've presumed you're selling something.

As I discussed in **Chapter 2. SALES FUNDAMENTALS** You need to get the prospects attention and engage them within the first 30 seconds of the call, with the hope that the call extends further. Remember, you've been given the first 30 seconds for free. However, it's up to you to earn further time credits with your prospects.

As you'll read in the next **Chapter 7. RESEARCH AND STRATEGY**, if you've done your research then you will know what (if any) connections you have to your prospects. Maybe you supply the same customer as they do? or you supply a local company that they know? or you share the same supplier? maybe you have shared contacts?

The point is, that within the first 30 seconds you can name drop and let them know you're calling them on the back of what you know. The stronger the name drop the more likely you'll be to use it and mention it early doors. If you don't name drop early doors, you'll be ready to mention it if the excuses start coming your way.

If you're given the "I'm busy" or "I'm just going into a meeting" excuse, you can still use their excuse (their tactic) against them. Some prospects will actually want you to assume that their excuse is a brush off, they want you to know they aren't interested but without saying so. Adopt a naive position and assume that they are busy and are about to go into a meeting (…by the way, some actually will be, but assume not many).

By adopting this naive position, you'll be letting your prospects know that you've not in any way assumed you're being brushed off. You'll apologise, not for calling (never do that), but for calling at an inconvenient time. The key now is NOT to ask the prospect "when is a good time to call again?" as you risk a further brush off, often with the 'send more information' excuse.

Suggest to the prospect when you'll call back, "Tomorrow at 10am" or "Thursday at 2pm", the key is for you to suggest the day and time, if the prospect doesn't want you to call (ever!) it's up to them to tell you so. If they push back on your suggested date, suggest a new date. Tell them you can speak at 10am any day next week other than Tuesday, as you're in a meeting. It's important that you don't give the impression you've got a completely free diary, you need them to know you're a busy person too, you get the gist.

The point here is that if you ask your prospects for a good time to call them back, you risk being brushed off. Just keep (gently) suggesting days and times until one sticks, or until the prospect says 'never'.

As you read earlier, if you've done your research, then it's always a good idea to throw in a name drop (if you haven't already) when suggesting your call back. Maybe the name drop is a local company to them or a customer they supply, or a company within the same industry, or someone they know personally. Whoever the name drop, it's important to throw the name in just before you suggest the date. As an example, "I'm speaking to (name drop) on Tuesday morning, I know you supply them, we do too. I'll call you afterwards at 10am if that's ok?" You obviously hadn't arranged a call with your customer, you wanted to get the name drop in with the hope that the prospect latches on to it.

In this example, it's important that you've done your research in advance of the call and you know which of their customers you supply too. Also, you actually then need to call your customer before you call the prospect on Tuesday morning. You can use this as an opportunity to ask them about the prospect and request that they provide a testimonial if your prospect requires one.

It's important for you to understand that when you told your prospect that you were calling your customer on Tuesday morning, it's because that's exactly what you intended to do if your prospect agreed to a call-back. Just because it wasn't already in your diary doesn't make you dishonest. It's your strategy to call customers prior to prospects if you have 'shared' customers or suppliers and the prospect warrants this much effort.

Of course, not all of your prospects will warrant the same level of research, focus and effort. For the ones that do, keep up the research and keep name dropping.

There is nothing more satisfying (other than a closed deal of course!) than a prospect going from an excuse to get you off the phone to then staying on the line for 20 minutes, either because of the name drop or because your research has led you to find wonderful touch points to speak about. This highlights how important the research was and how valuable name dropping is. It also provides evidence that the prospect wasn't that busy and the meeting they was about to go into either wasn't happening or wasn't that immediate, you'll use this experience for future calls with new prospects.

Top tip: If you can keep your prospects away from being able to provide you with these excuses then great. However, if you receive them then use their tactics against them whilst at the same time doing as much as you can to ensure that when you call back your prospect is more responsive.

I've never heard of your company

I always think this is a great opportunity to then say, "That's why I'm calling, to let you know who we are and what we can offer you". You need to be quick to name drop too, as it will quickly highlight that although they haven't heard of your company there are plenty of other businesses (many that they might know) that are your customers. Customer testimonials will highlight how well respected and well-known your company is too.

You can also use this as an opportunity to highlight any awards, accreditations or articles within the press. This will further highlight that although they haven't heard of your company, you're well-known within your industry and within the business community.

If you ever receive this objection, you could also say "that's what the competition like you to say, as they know when we do appear on your radar, we often win your business".

Like with many of these objections it's your ability to be inventive and creative with your responses that will determine your success over time. There is no set list for these responses, you'll have many already in your sales locker and you'll create many too.

Top tip: 'Dare to be different' and try out new responses. Use your own time in your own headspace to play around with various calls, situations and objections, then when you're back at work try them out for real.

We only deal with local suppliers

If you're local then of course, that was easy! If you're not, then consider why do some prospects say this. Surely, most don't actually mean this. Again, I'd suggest they will say this to get you off the phone so use their tactics against them.

Ask them if all their customers are local? surely not. If so, why do they then take this position with suppliers.

Ask your prospects what would happen if their customers all had the same view, the world of business would be a much smaller place and their customer base would be much smaller too.

If you've done your research, then you will already know what customers they supply, and you'll already know where these customers are located around the UK.

Once you've made your point, enquire why they have this view. If they aren't forthcoming, suggest a few reasons...

Is it because of service and response times?

Is it because of price?

Is it because they like to see people face to face more often?

...whatever the reason you can overcome all of this and more.

Explain that some of your loyal customers initially took this position when you first contacted them, and now after many years are glad they changed their views.

Explain and reassure (gently) that there isn't a valid reason why any prospect should only want to deal with a local provider. Not only does it limit what's available to them, but it also sends out the wrong message to their customers and staff.

Top tip: You'll often find this isn't true! So, play the game, be naive and get them to consider your valid points, as you're actually highlighting to them how contradictory their position is. If it is true, your points will strike an even stronger chord.

It's not something we're looking at right now

If the prospect already uses the products & services you provide and is out of contract and eligible to renew, then you need to be reiterating why they should be speaking to you now. Maybe they can save money by renewing which in turn means they'll potentially be losing money every month they don't renew.

You need to look at what's different between what they've currently got and what you can offer. Highlight the areas of strength, where your products & services are more productive and more efficient etc.

As per **Chapter 2. SALES FUNDAMENTALS** you'll recall that you need to be selling your features & benefits as the bells and whistles of your products & services. You need to understand why your prospect is not interested at this time and persuade and encourage them to reconsider.

If it's a time thing, then reassure them that the process won't take long. Whatever the reason, you need to persuade, encourage and convince them that they will be pleased they provided you an opportunity to help and quote them.

You'll often hear 'we're' rather than 'I'm'. If they say we're not looking at this right now, then you need to understand if this is a company opinion and if so, why? If they say I'm not looking at this right now, you need to understand why? You'll often find it's them and not the company no matter what they tell you.

You'll often find that the reason (more likely excuse) for this objection is that they are too busy, if so, acknowledge this and ask them if they weren't so busy would they have discussed this with you. They will be relaxed that you've accepted defeat and will often say yes, as they think you'll soon be ending the call. This is important, as you'll read in the top tip.

Top tip: It's a common theme now to use their excuses against them. After receiving acknowledgement that they'd have spoken to you if they wasn't so busy, ask your prospect how long 'right now', 'not at this time', 'currently' or 'at this present time' means and be positive with them that this small window of 'being busy' will soon be over and you can then pick up conversations with them about your products & services as they agreed they'd speak to you when things are a little quieter.

If they can't establish a time to call back, suggest one not too far away, let them know you'll connect with them on LinkedIn and/or send them an email. Now end the call saying, "speak soon". You need to be remembered, send them a LinkedIn message and/or an email thanking them for agreeing to a call when things aren't so busy. Confirm the date (or timeframe) you said you'd call again and give them a brief (very brief) overview of some highlights to you, your business and your products & services. If you can, give them some bait on the hook that might attract their attention, and a name drop or two.

Your message needs be talking about the future and not now, such as:

"I look forward to discussing x, y and z with you".

"I'm hopeful our current offers will extend to our next call".

The point is you didn't get a chance on the last call to explain what products & services you offer in any great detail and you couldn't speak about the features & benefits either. So, by dropping these things into a 'future call' message, you're actually wanting and intending for them to read it now. They might contact you back sooner? or it'll help on your next call when you remind them of the last call you had with them.

There are so many other pre-quoting objections and I'll include these in the future books I'll write. Like most chapters in this book, there are many topics that warrant further exploration and explanation, I'll include these subjects and more in future books. As this book was written in 2019, you might find that these future books are already a reality now, written and ready to purchase. Go search for them! thanks in advance.

POST QUOTING OBJECTIONS & EXCUSES

These are the objections and excuses you might receive once you've presented your quotes to your prospects.

You've generated a new lead, you've got passed the initial sales pitch, you've had your requirements call or meeting, you've got that all important DIP (deal in principle) and its now decision day.

These are just a few of the objections or excuses you might receive. It's important to remember any of the objections or excuses you overcame pre-quoting, as these responses will continue to support you now.

Price

Price will be a regular objection unless you counter this beforehand.

Some buyers will be on auto pilot once you've quoted and will ask you to lower your price, or even suggest you're out on price even if you're not.

If you don't establish price expectations early within the quoting process, you'll often end up at an impasse.

It can often be a game of cat and mouse where the buyer doesn't want to reveal what they're paying or are willing to pay, whilst at the same time you as the seller don't want to reveal the best price you can offer.

As you will read in **Chapter 6. INFLUENCER OR DECISION MAKER?** If your prospect is an influencer and not the decision maker, you need to understand how motivated they are in terms of price as there may be other factors that will get your deal over the line.

If your prospect tells you that your price is more expensive than the current supplier or than what they've been quoted elsewhere, you'll need to make a decision. Either, lower your price if you're commercially able to, or, convince and persuade them why your overall package is better.

Consider, they might be trying it on? and haven't received a lower price.

The problem with lowering your price too quickly or lowering your price at all, is that it could weaken your position and prove that you didn't offer your best price first time. If you're able to lower your price and you choose to do so, then you will need to find a good reason as to why you're now able to do this.

You could say you negotiated hard with your boss on behalf of the prospect, or, you could say you accessed a fighting fund that was specifically created for acquiring customers from the competition, …you get the gist. Whatever your reason, you need to be creative and convincing.

DO NOT lower your price before you've got a commitment from your prospect that you will secure their business by doing so. Tell your prospect that if you go back to your boss and persuade them to lower the price you will need an assurance from them that you'll close the deal.

You'll also need to establish the price beforehand, if you're matching a price or you're being asked to beat a price then you'll need to agree on the figure that you'll take back to your boss for approval.

If you know your own commercials, know what wriggle room you have in your deal and know what your boss will agree to then you'll know what price to work towards. You might not even need to speak to the boss, this was just the pretence you had to play out in this scenario.

However, if you've offered the best price you can without any further wriggle room, then champion this price and wrap everything else around it including service.

As I said in **Chapter 2. SALES FUNDAMENTALS** Section **9. SELL YOU AND YOUR COMPANY**, you need to ensure that you add as much value to what you and your company will offer / provide them.

Again, this is where customer testimonials are essential, trust and reassurance are so important.

Top tip: Make price the least important topic of conversation. Sell on everything else first before discussing price. Sell you and your company, sell the products & services and sell the features & benefits. Discuss savings, efficiencies and set great expectations for the future. Sell on trust and reassurance using your customer testimonials.

By the time you get to talk about price (towards the end of your pitch), you want to have done enough to justify their decision to say 'yes' to your deal, it might actually stop their objection to price.

Fear of Change

This again will often depend on whether you're dealing with the influencer or decision maker. It'll be your job to work out if they really fear change or if they just want to stay with their current provider.

For some prospects, it's all too much work and effort to move suppliers so they'll use excuses to convince themselves and others that change is bad.

Now, you won't often be told they fear change, you'll be told they are happy with their current provider or another excuse. For those prospects that do fear change it's your job to convince and persuade them why change can be good and why a change to you, your company and your products & services is the right move for them. Understand what's causing this fear, this doubt, this reluctance to move. It might be past bad experiences, if so, this isn't fair on you. You'll need to persuade your prospects why they shouldn't tarnish everyone with the same brush. Again, customer testimonials will provide trust and reassurance.

When providing customer testimonials and an overview of the businesses you work with, you'll have the opportunity to explain that for many they too had a fear of change and had been with their current suppliers for years. You'll reassure your prospects that these customers (your customers) are 'so happy' they've provided you glowing testimonials.

You should also use this excuse against them. If their customers also initially took this position, they'd still be prospects and they'd have a much smaller customer base. They encourage their prospects to change and it evidently works well.

Ask your prospect how their salespeople overcome this objection with their prospects? For many, they won't know as they don't work in sales but that's fine you weren't looking for an answer you were just making a wider point.

Let your prospects know, that fear of change works beautifully for the current supplier of course, maybe they've planted this seed in the first place?

Top tip: I often use the phrase 'better the devil you know' when a prospect fears change. As by its very nature it's suggesting that their current provider is the best of a bad lot! (devil). Of course, you're not actually saying this, you're simply suggesting that for some customers they feel that it's 'better the devil you know' when it comes to either staying with a current provider or moving to a new one.

I would paint a picture of a new provider (me) that would set the bar much higher in terms of service, trust and customer experience (angel).

I'd also reiterate that it's not fair to tarnish all suppliers the same. Are they the best of a bad lot themselves? Surely not.

It's a No. I don't know why, it's not my decision

You should have already established before you quoted if your prospect is the influencer or decision maker and as such you should have already requested to your prospect if you can meet the decision maker directly to present your quote. I discussed this in chapter 2.

I've dedicated the next **Chapter 6. INFLUENCER OR DECISION MAKER** to this very subject.

If you were unable to achieve this and had to provide your quote to the influencer, then there are further steps you could have taken prior to quoting that will at the very least ensure you're told the reason behind the decision makers 'no' decision.

Consider, that some influencers will use this objection as an easy way to stop negotiations with you and further communication, especially if they had an agenda all along of not agreeing to a new deal with you (or anyone in fact).

Prior to quoting and at the point where you're told you won't have the opportunity to present your quote to the decision maker you can then ask how you'll receive feedback from the decision maker if their decision is no. This is an obvious answer, as your prospect (the influencer) will say they will pass the feedback on to you themselves. This now means that if the decision maker says no, the influencer won't be able to shut up shop and say they 'don't know why'. They assured you beforehand that you'll know the reasons why if you're unsuccessful and you'll remind them of this.

Of course, if the influencer had provided a reassurance and commitment via a DIP that if you provided this, that and the other you'd have a deal you can push back if the reason being given contradicts what you've quoted, and the DIP agreed.

You can also choose to take the risk and contact the decision maker directly. A risky move, as if unsuccessful you'll undoubtedly lose the opportunity to quote them again in the future as you'll have alienated yourself to the influencer. Also, even if successful in terms of turning the decision maker around, you might still lose, as the decision maker often doesn't want to undermine the influencer.

However, sales is sometimes about taking risks and it can pay off. It all comes down to how great your deal is and how wrong the decision not to agree a new deal with you is, in the eyes of the decision maker.

My advice would be to do all you can way before you've quoted to get in front of the decision maker, there's lots of ways to achieve this. At the very least, you can be subtle, maybe you connect with the decision maker on LinkedIn with a personal message thanking them in advance for considering your proposal, or, like and comment on a social media post they've sent. Be subtle, the hope is you attract their attention with the hope that they then realise you're the same person that's quoting

176

their business. Of course, they might not even be aware that you're quoting and/or might not care.

Any contact you receive back is a good thing, an accepted LinkedIn invitation is great. My advice would be to not further engage directly with the decision maker until after they say yes or no. However, consider that anything you post, like or share on LinkedIn they will now see, if they are active on this platform of course. If the decision maker sees you liking their company posts etc this will not only show you're helping promote their company, but it also keeps you in the decision makers thoughts. The hope is they check you out further and look at your profile, recommendations etc.

As I discussed in chapter 2 and I'll discuss again in **Chapter 7. RESEARCH AND STRATEGY**, you must ensure your social media profiles promotes you in the way you want to be seen by your prospects. The strategy you now adopt is one that ensures you post content that further promotes you in a positive light, especially with the decision maker in mind.

When quoting ask the influencer if they would allow you to copy the decision maker into the email, if you email your quote to them. Just say, that it at least provides you with a sense of inclusion with them as you're not able to directly present the proposal to them. If by this time, you're already connected to them via social media you can intimate that it feels right to include them.

You could choose to play the naive card and copy the decision maker into the email anyway. A risky move but as long as you don't reference the decision maker into the body of the email you can be naive and suggest that you thought that's what was required. In the end, what's the issue? especially if you provide positive comments about the influencer within the email, everyone wants to look good in front of their boss! You can suggest the email would have ended up in their inbox anyway, so you've saved the influencer a job.

You could also use their tactics against them, if you feel that the influencer hasn't influenced your deal enough to the decision maker, or, you feel that the influencer has an agenda and doesn't want to proceed with your deal. Ask the prospect, if it was their decision would they have agreed a new deal with you. You'll sometimes find you'll receive a 'yes' as the prospect assumes you've accepted defeat and they want to end the call giving you a little confidence boost and to get you off the phone. If they say yes, then suggest that you work together on changing the decision makers mind. Make the point that you can't see the point in the prospect doing what they've done throughout this process to then not be listened to by the decision maker. If the prospect goes with this sentiment with a 'hey ho, what can you do...that's life' attitude but still with a tone of someone that wants the call to end shortly, suggest that you make contact with the decision maker directly.

Whether you do or don't contact the decision maker is up to you. Yes, it's risky and yes you could alienate yourself with any future interactions. However, you might find the decision maker didn't have the full facts, the influencer did have an agenda and the decision maker is responsive.

As I've said throughout this book, 'dare to be different' and take risks from time to time. You just need to ensure that you get it right far more than you get it wrong, and you don't let the 'knocks', hit you too hard when you get it wrong, as trust me you will now and again.

You could just accept defeat and wait for another opportunity in the future, to quote the prospect again. However, you might find you end up in the same situation as now, then wishing you'd took a risk the last time you quoted.

There are so many permutations to these scenarios, and I can't cover them all now.

In summary, be sceptical of all 'no' decisions from influencers, assume nothing, take risks and dare to be different.

Top tip: Get in front of the decision maker!

We're staying with our current provider

As per **Chapter 2. SALES FUNDAMENTALS** if you've already got a DIP (deal in principle) in place, then this objection will surprise you if you've done what's required, as the prospect had already told you that if you did this, that and the other you'd have a deal.

If you've not done what's required, you'll need to understand quickly where you've fallen short with a view to overturning their decision.

If you're given an objection (or excuse) then it's a little late to the party but you need to overcome it, and quickly. You might have already overcome this objection when pre-quoting too, so remind them again.

Beware, some prospects will use your quote to get their current provider to match or beat your deal. This might have always been their agenda and might be a policy they adopt each and every time a renewal date arrives. You need to weaken the current supplier's position by questioning why it takes a 'new' supplier like you to get them to improve their deal. Surely, they should respect the fact they are the current supplier and ensure they are the benchmark for all things price, service etc. If anything, it should have been you that was looking to beat or match the deal they offered!

It's important to understand if the current supplier had already quoted and they amended the quote offered in response to your quote. If so, you need to challenge this and suggest they should have quoted you their best quote first time, just like you did.

You need to also question the motives and/or agenda of the prospect by allowing this policy to continue. What if no one else bothers to ever quote the prospect, does this mean they stay on a poor deal? or does the prospect go searching for others to quote just so they can get a better deal from the current supplier?…it sounds crazy I know, but this bad practice does happen.

Before you quote the prospect, you need to be prepared that this might happen. Be clear with the prospect that you will quote your 'best deal first time' and suggest they ensure their current supplier and others do the same. You can follow on to say that you're amazed how often other suppliers improve their deal when they get wind of what you're offering. Sure, this highlights what a great deal you provide but also highlights that other suppliers are either holding back, being greedy or taking liberties.

For some, they simply can't get near what you can offer so will adapt other strategies to convince the customer to stay with them. Fear of change comes to mind, or bad mouthing your company. It does happen I'm afraid. Further highlight how your company's retention levels are fantastic because you ensure that the 'best deal first time' policy is continued throughout the lifetime of all your customer relationships, your company continues to set the benchmark and your deals are not governed by what others offer.

Top tip: You should already know before you quote what your prospect likes and would change about their current supplier. So, use the 'would changes' to strengthen your argument why they should move suppliers to you. You'll need to remind them what they said they'd change and remind them that doing nothing guarantees they'll only get the same. Reiterate that you built your quote to ensure that you gave them the same (if not better) 'likes' and also gave them the 'changes' they'd like. If they do what they've always done, they'll get what they've always had.

In summary…in the end, it's all about results.

Are you losing opportunities and/or deals because of the objections and excuses you're receiving and your inability to overcome them? Hopefully, the advice and tips I've provided give you some ideas on how to overcome these. You need to allow objections to work for you, rather than against you.

The more you think about your prospect's objections and excuses and the tactics they might deploy the better you'll be at overcoming them as you'll be so much better prepared.

If you've ever heard someone say "buyers are better than sellers" it's because they want you to consider that buyers often spend more time thinking about their tactics towards sellers. This saying is absolute nonsense of course, as it's pitting buyers and sellers against each other.

In sales, a good seller will often sell to a buyer. A bad seller will rarely sell to a buyer and will further enhance the myth that buyers are better than sellers. To be considered a good seller, you need to be closing deals of course, hitting your targets and earning good commissions. You'll only do this consistently if you learn to overcome objections.

Also, as you read in **Chapter 2. SALES FUNDAMENTALS** there are 'good sales practices' that need to be adopted to ensure you're a real success in sales.

You'll notice I didn't say good or bad buyers, that's because there aren't any. Yes, some are better than others in terms of negotiating the best deals for their businesses. Some are proactive, some are reactive, and some are neither. Some are tough, and some are soft. Some are efficient, and some are lazy. Some have an agenda, and some don't. In the end just focus on being a good seller, adopt a core set of sales fundamentals and you'll sell to all types of buyers.

Now, at risk of repeating myself...research is essential! The more you know about your prospects the better, it'll get your prospects on the phone and it'll make your conversations so much easier. You'll build rapport, trust and interest in you, your company and your products & services. The more you know about your competition the better too, as you'll dig up a whole treasure trove of information that can work for you and against them. Again, to reiterate, be gentle and smart with this information, you're promoting your strengths to weaken their position. Good research takes time, effort and a desire to connect the dots.

In **Chapter 7. RESEARCH AND STRATEGY**, I'll explain this valuable resource in greater detail.

Chapter 6. INFLUENCER OR DECISION MAKER?

It's essential that you clarify early doors if your contact is the decision maker or the influencer. Of course, the decision maker is the person ideally that you want & need to be speaking to, but if this isn't possible then you must understand the role of the influencer.

Influencer

There are different types of influencer, and their influence on the decision maker and to championing your proposal might be strong or weak.

An influencer can be motivated by many things, and their appetite to get your deal over the line will differ with each and every influencer you speak to or meet. It's your job to find out what their appetite, agenda and motivation is for buying your products & services and their desire to change suppliers if they already use your products & services via a competitor. Whilst doing this, you're obviously required to persuade and appeal to your influencer, create and/or encourage an appetite, help set the agenda and motivate them towards influencing the decision maker to buy your products & services.

You need to know the characteristics, mindset and agenda of your influencer. Consider these things when interacting with them:

It's not their money!

If it's not their money then ask yourself, why will they work hard to save their employer money? Sure, they might be good at their job and diligent in ensuring they are safeguarding their employers interests, but this will be your job to find out.

When quoting influencers that aren't driven by savings and bottom lines, then get the balance right and ensure you appeal to things that are important to them too. For instance, if they are more interested in service levels and KPI's etc, then focus on that. However, be aware that the decision maker might be money driven and the bottom line /

ROI (return on investment) is their top priority. It's about getting the balance right and ensuring your proposal appeals to the influencer AND the decision maker. If they are both in tune and singing from the same song sheet, then great!

If the decision maker is guided by a very 'influential' influencer then even better, as long as you've got the influencer on your side championing you, your company and your products & services. If this is the case, you'll find the influencer knows how to appeal to the decision maker and will use their influence to get the decision you both want.

Why should they and why will they encourage change?

If they are happy with their current supplier, then why would they want to help enact a change? even if you know you're offering a better price and are committed to offering a better service. It's your job to find out what their appetite is for change.

If they've been working in their current position for a while, use your investigative skills to find out what changes have previously been enacted by them and why. You're trying to establish what their appetite has previously been for change and what their agenda is now, if they have one.

They might not want to enact change and might have a 'better the devil you know' attitude?

They might be continually pitched for their business and their phone and emails might be bombarded by salespeople?

They might have a bad perception of you and/or other suppliers? This is why you need to 'dare to be different' and appreciate their current position /stance with a view to chaining their thoughts, feelings and opinions. You can use their lethargy of not changing suppliers against them, especially if you find that their current provider isn't very good.

Now let me be clear, don't go looking for their current provider to be bad and don't insinuate they are without evidence. Be respectful and appreciate that there are good and bad suppliers elsewhere, and there will be plenty of good salespeople just like you.

Their current supplier might be wonderful, and the influencer might like them if no change has been enacted for a while. It's your job to understand and appreciate what your prospect likes about their current supplier and ensure you are better. Words are cheap, you'll need to prove to them just how great you are, how great your company is and how great your products & services are. Customer testimonials are essential for this, there's no better way of proving your worth than your existing customers recommending you.

Of course, it's ideal if it can be proven that their current supplier isn't very good, the deal they currently receive isn't competitive and the service levels they receive are inadequate in comparison to yours. What you don't want to do is be all "na-nana-na-naa" as this will get you nowhere other than to alienate you to the influencer.

If their current supplier is as bad as you hope, the facts will speak for themselves. The hope is that the influencer has been naive in assuming everything was fine and not considering new suppliers, they'll soon realise this if you're careful and considerate in how you help them come to this realisation.

If the influencer is fairly new to their role then this might be a positive as they might want to enact change and save money, to highlight why they are good at their job? Saving money might also be the thing that highlights why their predecessors were bad at their jobs? If this is the case, you can assist the prospect in finding fault and making them look better to their new employer, you can enact change together. On the other hand, they might want to settle in and not ruffle any feathers or create more work for themselves?

The influencer might be new to purchasing and new to the products & services you're offering. If so, there is an opportunity to help, educate and guide them. You can empower them with knowledge that they can take back to the decision maker and take back to their current supplier. It's great when you can get an influencer asking questions to their current supplier that have been guided & prompted by you. Especially if you know the answer they'll receive will help and empower you, whilst at the same time weakening the current suppliers position.

If the influencer was previously employed in a similar role elsewhere then they may have previous contacts and suppliers that they are used to working with and like? Be respectful and appreciate they'll give these people an opportunity. It's your job to use your sales skills to persuade, encourage and influence them that although these people are good, you're so much better.

You need to know what part the influencer plays in the day to day stuff, as you'll be able to understand, appreciate and empathise with this and then sell on the basis you can assist and improve things for them in terms of customer service and support. Of course, you need to be able to back this up and ensure if successful you do indeed provide this level of service. Again, customer testimonials will help you provide reassurance to your prospects.

The points I'm making are simply to highlight that there are many types of influencer and we obviously shouldn't prejudice them all, but in the same way we can't be naive to think they are all going to do what's required in terms of giving you every opportunity of securing a new deal. It's your job to do your research, ask the right questions (many of which you might not have asked before, because you didn't think it was necessary) and build a rapport with the influencer. In doing so you'll be in a better position to know, understand and appreciate what their appetite, agenda and motivations are.

For the influencers that want change and that like you and your quote, encourage them to allow you to join & support them when they present your proposal to the decision maker. You'll then provide back up to each other and ensure the change happens.

For the influencers that have an agenda and an intention of staying with their current providers, you'll need to 'Influence the influencer'.

Some influencers are actually the decision makers

Consider that sometimes, the influencers are actually the decision makers, they just don't want you know to know that.

Why? Well, it makes it easier for them if they decide to say 'no'. They'll say it was out of their hands and it wasn't their decision. Good research and great questioning can often help you determine if they are indeed the decision makers, or far more influential than they are letting on. If they are, you don't need to let them know you know, play the game.

As you read in **Chapter 5. OBJECTION HANDLING** you can use their objections & excuses to your advantage.

Decision Maker

The decision maker is the person you probably spend most of your time considering in sales and hopefully the person you are speaking to and in front of most of the time. But, of course, this isn't always the case.

Can you get in front of the decision maker? As you'll then obviously be in direct control of how your quote is presented and you'll know first-hand what the decision makers appetite is for change.

The decision maker is just that, the person that signs on the dotted line, the person that decides the 'yes or no' and the person that decides if you have a closed sale or not.

Much of what I wrote in this chapter for the influencer, applies to the decision maker too. Of course, decision makers aren't always directors or shareholders and indeed everyone has their own reasons, motivations and agendas when it comes to buying products & services.

If the people you are directly speaking to are able to say 'yes' and agree your deal without any other person's authority, then they are obviously the decision makers and the best people for you to be speaking to and negotiating with.

(Q) How often are you speaking to decision makers?

Chapter 7. RESEARCH AND STRATEGY:
Knowledge with a plan of action

Research is a key part of your lead generation strategy and a key ingredient you'll utilise in gaining more sales. Knowledge really is power, the more you know about the people you're talking to and the businesses they work for the better.

Research will help you source new leads and target great prospects.

Research will help you get your foot in the door, help you break the ice, help you build rapport and help you close more deals.

Research and strategy will support and strengthen your sales pitch.

Research will help you get one step ahead of the competition and more importantly one step closer to your prospects before you've even spoken to them.

There are so many tools available to assist your research, there really is no excuse to not empower yourself. Of course, some prospects warrant more research than others and some sales roles require little or lots of research. It all comes down to what you sell and the types of prospects you are looking to attract.

Your products & services might be quick wins, with low value or they might be high value with a methodical approach required, they might be a mix of all of this?

This chapter will include an overview of the types of research information available and how best to utilise it. I'll leave it to you to determine how much of this you do and how much of this is relevant or suited to your sales role, the products & services you sell and the types of prospects you're looking to attract.

It's great having lots of wonderful research info, but ineffective if you don't know how to use it, and benefit from it. This is where strategy comes in. Research and strategy are a wonderful double act, they work in sync and complement each other.

The plan with this chapter, is to get your research juices flowing and to ensure that research and strategy becomes a key part of your sales role. Like with most of the chapters in this book, there is so much more I could have written on this important subject. I'll write a future book specifically about research and strategy. This book was written in 2019, so if you're reading this in 2020 or beyond this book might already be available, go take a look and find out.

For now, let's look at a few of the various tools and methods you should be using.

Company website

There is a whole load of valuable information on a company's website.

Let's start with a typical home page, there's loads of info on this page and it's the central part of any website with links for you to navigate the site. The home page provides you an instant snapshot of the business, you'll see the company logo and the company brand. The look and feel are so important.

Some websites encourage you to click on certain tabs, links or images. If so, do that, follow the journey they prefer.

Some homepages include customer testimonials, customer logos, awards and accreditations. This all helps you paint a picture of your prospect. You can also use their customer information and contact those customers as new prospects, you might also find that some are already in your current prospect list or even better they are an existing customer.

When you're contacting these new prospects, you'll need to also mention the current prospect that led you to them. Name dropping is essential, you might prefer to wait until you've quoted your prospect before you start contacting their customers, or, even better wait until you've closed the deal! What's important is that you paint a picture to your new prospect that you've seen them on your current prospects website as you're currently quoting them, or you've recently won their business. You can adopt this strategy with all your prospects and existing customers.

Of course, you should have already asked / been asking for recommendations from your customers, but this doesn't stop you from sourcing new prospects from their websites. Start looking more closely at your existing customers websites, there is a treasure trove of info.

Each pitch you then make you'll be able to say you're calling because you supply (name drop) and I know you're a customer of theirs…such an easy and fun strategy, it keeps things interesting too. As you read in chapter 2, and as you'll read in chapter 8, all prospects are thinking 'who are you and what do you want' when you call them, so to have a reason immediately like this makes life so much easier for you.

Of course, what's also great about this strategy is that you'll have your customer to back you up and provide testimony too if required. Your customer can also steer you in the right direction and maybe even let you know the best contact to speak too.

From the home page you'll often see links / tabs including:

Contact us

If the prospect is already within your database, this is a good chance to ensure you've got the correct telephone number and address, there might be multiple numbers, even DDI's or mobile numbers. You'll see if the company has more than one address, maybe they have a HQ and other offices? This might widen your opportunity.

You might see an email structure, such as: firstname.surname@businessname.co.uk or firstinitial.surname@businessname.com.

This is beneficial as you can assume (for now) that your prospects email address follows this pattern, if you don't already have it.

About us

What a great way to get to know the company you're calling.

You might learn what year they started trading, what their journey has been, how many employees they have, what customers they supply, what awards they've won, and accreditations acquired.

You'll often learn things that you didn't know before, even though you might have been calling this prospect for a while. Remember, the about us section is what 'they' want you to know about them. There will be a tone, flavour and message within this text and/or imagery…you need to then mirror this when you communicate with your prospect.

These extra snippets of info can often help you change your strategy, approach and sales pitch.

Meet the team

Meet the team is a great way to get a snapshot of the key people in the business. You'll often see pictures too, it's great to put a face to a name.

If it's a new prospect you might see who heads up the various departments, and you might also see their contact details too.

Some businesses like to add some personality to this section, so you might acquire some important personal info about your prospect, something quirky about them or simply things they like, don't like or care about.

You might find that you interact with another person in the business as a stepping stone to the influencer or decision maker you actually need to be speaking to. On LinkedIn (for instance) you'll see where these people have previously worked, where they went to school and which connections they share with you.

Products & services

It's important to know what products & services your prospects provide.

It's not enough to want to know if they use 'your' products & services, or if they have a requirement to use them now or in the future. You need to know what your prospects do, as it will show you're interested, and you care when you're communicating with them. You will also then be able to see where your own products & services fit within their business and the level of importance they play.

New opportunities often arise once you understand what their business does, maybe your business provides other products & services that you can also sell to them? Maybe you supply existing customers that you can introduce to your prospects that can help them, buy from them or sell to them?

Latest news

Latest news often provides a great insight to the business your speaking too, what a great way to know and appreciate what's happening within the business you're prospecting. Remember, it's what their business wants you to know.

You'll read about growth plans, new office locations, recruitment drives, work in the local community, awards won, new customers acquired, charity work, sponsorships. There's so much you can learn and plenty of info you can shoehorn into your conversations with your prospects. Remember, you're going to want and need to build rapport with your prospects and you're going to want to break the ice too.

Your prospects will also appreciate that you've took the time to do your research too.

Our customers

This is a great way to see who your prospect supplies.

You'll get a snapshot of the types of businesses they supply and the size too. You might see recognisable brands, local businesses or businesses in the same industry as you.

You might see your own existing customers or current prospects, if so, you can contact these businesses with a view to helping you open doors and/or provide valuable information.

You can also contact these businesses and add them to your prospects list. When you speak to them you can then shoehorn in your relationship to your current prospect.

Customer testimonials

As with the 'our customers' section, you'll often find customer testimonials too.

These might be across the whole of the company's website including their homepage, or, might be within a specific section.

The great thing about customer testimonials, is that you can get an insight into why their customers purchased from them. You can then use this within your sales pitch and strategy.

You might also see the name of the person that provided the testimonial, so you can pitch them directly, name dropping of course.

When you communicate back with your current prospect you can say that your ultimate ambition is to not only supply them your products & services but to also receive a glowing testimonial similar to the ones on their company website. You can direct them to your own company website, where they can see similar glowing testimonials that mirror the same values, care and service. Of course, ensure you do indeed have glowing testimonials on your company website and ensure they are up to date too.

Customer testimonials can also provide a valuable insight into how your prospects acquire new business and manage their own customers; you can use the same tones when pitching your prospects.

Social media (icons)

It's important for you to research each of the various social media platforms that your prospects use. You can learn so much!

For a start, (on the likes of Instagram and Twitter) you can see how many followers they have and how frequently they might be using social media. If they have a large audience and you eventually close a deal with them, you might persuade them to announce your win on their social media, raising your businesses profile, and yours too.

The content being posted is valuable too, as you'll often learn about their company culture, success stories, charity work etc, you can ride the wave of these stories and use it to get your foot in the door, build rapport and generate a new lead.

Social media often gives you an insight into the people and the personalities within their business. The businesses with smaller followers will make it easier for you to see if you know anyone following them or being followed by them. You'll be surprised by how many times you see an existing customer or someone you know following or being followed by your prospects.

On LinkedIn, it's always advisable to connect with your prospects. You'll already be able to see if you have any shared connections with your prospects or connections that can introduce you. I've called many existing customers and asked them how they know my prospects to then learn that the connection is so strong they actually introduced me & opened the door for me. Let me be clear, if a door can be easily opened for me rather than me battering it down myself, I'll take the easy and smarter option every time.

You can also consider following the company yourself. Of course, you'll receive their posts, and you'll be able to retweet, share, comment and like too. This might get you noticed by your prospects.

If your prospect also uses social media personally, consider following them too. Remember, as I've said before, you must ensure that your personal social media highlights the best of you.

If your business uses social media, then speak to your marketing team and ask them to follow your prospects business and the prospect themselves. Your prospect might follow back or log onto your website. The point is, you're staying on their radar.

The more you can do to interact with your prospects the more you'll be noticed, thought about, talked about and considered for new opportunities.

Newsletters

Newsletters are a great way to source lots of information about the businesses you are prospecting. Similar to the info you'll receive on social media and within latest news, you'll often find much more detailed information as it'll often cover a monthly or a quarterly period.

If you need to subscribe to read these, then do so. You'll then receive them in your inbox as soon as each newsletter has been issued. Even if your prospect isn't eligible yet for your products & services, sign up now so you can start your interactions with your prospects in advance of the opportunity.

In summary, of course there is so much more to learn from a company's website, but this should give you the encouragement to spend more time looking at this valuable resource.

Social Media (and social selling)

Now, I've covered some of this within the last section, but let's expand this further from a research & strategy perspective.

I'm going to focus on LinkedIn, as in my opinion this is currently (as of 2019) one of the best research tools you'll have for business sales. Of course, I can only discuss LinkedIn based on what's available in 2019 as of course over time features and settings will change.

There are some wonderfully talented LinkedIn experts available to help you and lots of great books written too. I would suggest you continue this journey of self-improvement and source these people and these books too. For now, I'll share with you my own insights, opinions and views.

If you're not already using LinkedIn, you really should be. LinkedIn is a professional networking site for employers, employees, influencers, entrepreneurs, buyers, sellers…you name it, many are on this platform.

Before you start to use LinkedIn as a great research & social selling tool, there's a bit of housekeeping to do. You should ensure you have a personal profile that reflects you in a positive light, includes your background, your interests, your awards and accreditations.

What would you like others to know about you?

What would you like others to think about you?

Your personal profile is your showcase page, your CV and your hello to the world.

Write a great bio, that incapsulates the essence of you.

Include a photo of yourself, so your prospects & customers can see what you look like and that you're not hiding in the shadows. It really does make a huge difference to put a face to a voice & name. This also helps you if you go to meet your prospects & customers, as a quick look beforehand helps you greet the right person, trust me they will be doing the same as you too!

Look at other people's profiles and find inspiration, if you spend enough time tweaking your profile, you'll end up with a showcase page to be proud of.

Now, it's time to build your network. You can import your contacts into LinkedIn and connect with those that are also using this platform. Ensure you personalise your invite to them, you're much more likely to then be accepted and it's the correct etiquette too.

Over time, you'll find a tone and message that will work best for you when connecting with prospects. As your network grows, you'll find your home page feed will become more varied and interesting with your connections various posts. You'll be able to like, comment and share on these posts.

You should now start to post content yourself. Ensue your posts are interesting and add value, of course you can promote your products & services but be smart and creative about how you do this. The key is to ensure that more often than not, you add value to others.

You can post good news stories, new customer acquisitions or where you are on your travels around the UK. You'll be able to let people know what you're selling and the value you offer, by posting this type of content. Let your personality shine through and people will want to know more about you and what you sell. Just get the balance right, as LinkedIn is a professional platform, too many personal posts and it will look like Facebook or Instagram, too many sales posts and people will switch off. Be yourself, share your views and opinions and add value as much as you can.

You can join groups and use hashtags to further expand your reach. You can use the hashtags to find topics of conversation that are suited to you.

LinkedIn is a great platform to research your prospects. Think of your own profile, the information you provided about yourself is what you wanted others to read and see. It's the same for your prospects, they'll often have provided their photo, job title, job description, personal bio, contact information, education, work experience, interests & hobbies, skills & endorsements and recommendations etc.

Of course, there are settings within LinkedIn that allow the user to restrict what others see, some will only allow their 1st connections access to their personal info, others will allow all users full access. Some users might choose to allow 1st and 2nd connections access to their full profile. Either way, the best way to ensure you receive the full information is to connect with them.

As I mentioned earlier within this chapter, personalise your invite to them with a short message. Beforehand, look at how many connections they have, if it's less than 500 you'll often see the number. More than 500 and you can assume any number thereafter as it doesn't show. If they don't have many connections, consider are they new to the platform or are they particular about who they connect with? Maybe they aren't active on the platform anymore?

You'll be able to see what (if any) shared connections you have with them; this is a great opportunity to ask your 1st connections how they know your prospects, and can they introduce you.

Once your invite has been accepted, do not instantly start pitching them your products & services. You'll often alienate yourself to them, if they use the platform regularly, they'll soon start to see your posts, likes, shares and comments. You'll soon start to get noticed by them, and you'll soon find opportunities to interact with them with a view to then discussing what you sell, the benefits you offer and the value you provide.

You'll often be able to click on the company name within their experience section and view their company page. This provides plenty of information about the company you're wanting to sell to, but also lets you research the other employees within the business that are also using LinkedIn. As I mentioned a moment ago, you'll be able to see if you're connected to anyone else and who of your 1st connections might be connected to people within the business too. This is a great way to call or direct message one of your 1st connections to ask them how they know your prospect with a view to asking them for an intro.

You can then do the same thing with the previous businesses they worked for. See who else might have worked at those businesses that you know or are connected to either directly or indirectly via another connection.

You can enter their school or university into the search bar and see if any of your 1st connections attended the same school / university at the same time.

Look at their posts, likes, shares and comments as it will provide valuable information to what they like, don't like, care about or are interested in. You can like, share and comment to these posts too.

Within the 'Interests' section, you'll see which groups they are connected to. You can join these groups too as another way to interact with them and be noticed by them.

For some, you'll also see their date of birth, remember they chose to provide this information. It's worth making a note of this date, as it's a great opportunity to support your interactions with them and grow your relationship by wishing them a 'happy birthday'. Once connected with them, you'll be reminded & prompted by LinkedIn to wish them a happy birthday.

LinkedIn is a great platform for research and a great for social selling too. You can attract new leads, acquire new customers and promote yourself and your business to a wider audience.

Like with many of the subjects I've written about within this book, there is so much more I could have written about re: research & social selling.

Social selling is changing the way we interact with one another and the way buyers & sellers do business, I'll write a future book about this important subject. For now, I've kept it 'old school' within this book as the sales fundamentals I've written about are as still relevant & required in order to build solid sales foundations.

Of course, LinkedIn is only one of a handful of social media platforms. As I discussed in **Chapter 2. SALES FUNDAMENTALS** It's advisable to search for your prospects & customers on the likes of Twitter, Instagram and Facebook etc as it will often reflect them differently, which is a great way to learn more about them personally and away from their work environment.

You'll see who they follow, what they like and dislike and what they care about. There is often more than enough content for you to paint a picture of them with a view to using this information strategically to build rapport, influence and persuade.

You'll find from time to time that your prospects will include their other social media handles within their contact details, if so, it makes the task of finding them much easier. Also, if you search their company's social media, you'll often find your prospects appear as followers. Of course, the larger the following the more difficult this becomes.

Again, as I've said before if you're going to connect with your prospects & customers on social media you must ensure that your profile and the content you post & share show you in your best light. If they don't you need to tidy this up, or, delete these accounts and start over. Buyers research sellers too, so bear this in mind when you're doing your own research.

Company information

There is plenty of company information available for you to research. As I've already mentioned there is plenty to research from their company website. However, there are also other resources too.

In the UK you can look on Companies House and see who the directors are, you'll see if they are directors of other businesses and past businesses they've worked at too.

You can get many details about a limited company online, including the registered address, date of incorporation, previous company names and the current and resigned officers. You can also see financial information, as of course the financial health and stability of your prospects & customers is important.

You can use search engines like google to research your contacts too, use their name and the place they live, or, their name and company name, be creative using the information you already know and see what the wonderful world of the internet throws back at you. You'll soon start to find information that you would never have known about. Often, you'll find links to other websites that provide valuable information. The more you dig the more chance you'll have of finding treasure.

You should know as much as possible about the company that you want to buy your products & services. Look for industry news, national and local news, in fact any news that can give you a better insight and understanding of them.

You need to know the journey the business has been on and what (if any) its future growth plans are. The opportunity today might be a much bigger opportunity in the future, this might determine what you offer them now? so you can grow with them.

The knowledge you'll acquire won't just come from research, each and every interaction you have with your prospects & customers will provide you with new information that if recorded within your CRM notes will play a vital role in your sales strategy.

In summary, I'll end this chapter as I started it…knowledge is power!

The more you know and learn about your prospects & customers (the people and the businesses) the better you'll be at building rapport and gaining trust & confidence. Research and strategy really is knowledge with a plan of action.

Chapter 8. SALES ROLES:
Telesales & Telemarketing, Field Sales and Account Management

Includes:

a) TELESALES & TELEMARKETING

b) FIELD SALES

c) ACCOUNT MANAGEMENT

There are lots of different sales roles in business sales.

For some, it's selling products & services over the phone and for others it's generating leads and booking appointments.

For some, it's 'life on the road' attending appointments and for others it's managing existing customers in or out of the office.

For some, it's inbound sales calls and for others it's outbound sales calls.

Some sales roles are a mix of all of this.

I'd advise that throughout your sales career you try various sales roles as this is the best way to determine what you're best at, what you most enjoy and where you're able to maximise your true potential both professionally and financially.

For some, they have a suitability to a defined specific role, for others they like to do the lot. Throughout my sales career I've done all sales roles. It's my ability to be adaptable to many sales environments that I believe has been a significant factor in terms of my success in sales.

When I first set up my telecoms business, I knew I'd have to do the lot and I did. I hit the phones, generated new leads, closed deals over the phone, booked myself appointments, attended meetings and closed deals. I managed the accounts I'd secured with a view to retaining their business, renewing their orders and attracting recommended business from them.

Of course, as my business grew, I quickly employed people to fulfil these various sales roles. I worked alongside the sales team and encouraged, motivated, supported, coached & mentored them. This is where my love of sales coaching began, watching salespeople flourish from the help, advice and support I give them is wonderful.

So, let's look at a few sales roles **(in brief).**

You might be currently doing one of these roles, or maybe you're considering moving from one to another? If you're already working in any of these roles, I'm sure lots will resonate with you.

If you're not yet working in sales, you might be considering what's the best role for you?

I'll provide a brief overview / flavour to these roles and also some advice in terms of what you can expect. I've included some tips and techniques too.

a) TELSALES & TELEMARKETING

Before I discuss the differences between the 2 roles, let's discuss the similarities.

Your job is to call prospects, source new leads and generate interest in your products & services. As I've mentioned earlier within this book, you'll often speak to the head of first impressions before speaking to your prospects, I'll cover this again in a moment.

You need to understand that if this is the first time you've called the prospect, then it's likely the prospect will be thinking who are you? and, what do you want?, not in a negative way, it's just a natural position to take when someone takes your call. It's your job to answer those 2 questions but in a way that will then provide you with more time credits, you don't want the prospect to cut the call short, which will happen if your intro isn't right.

As I've mentioned in previous chapters, when you're making telephone calls to new prospects, play a game where the prospect has time credits that they'll provide you if you're doing well. The first 30 seconds comes for free; it's already been given to you by each and every prospect. Visualising this in itself will help you, you'll be less inclined to think that you won't be well received.

However, further time credits can now only be given to you by the prospect. You'll often find that after your initial 20 to 30 seconds, it's likely you'll receive a further 30 to 60 seconds time credit from the prospect if your intro is good and they understand a little as to why you're calling.

It's now your job to establish some common ground, build rapport and understand their requirements. You obviously won't achieve all of this

210

in 60 to 90 seconds, so you'll need to be rewarded with more time credits.

Your third time credit is key, it will either extend the call past 5 minutes or you'll be told to call back at a more convenient time. Beware of being asked to call back too often, as this pattern will mean prospects are fobbing you off and getting you off the phone.

Of course, timing is key. It might be an inconvenient time for the prospect as they weren't expecting your call. If so, great, the next call should be more convenient because you'll agree the day/time with them. If you're smart, you'll also book the call into your mutual diaries via a calendar invite (or something similar) so there's an expectation for you both on the day and time.

As you read in **Chapter 5. OBJECTION HANDLING** you'll receive plenty of excuses and it's your ability to overcome them and use them to your advantage that will often determine your success or failure when in telesales and telemarketing.

Remember, when you're making outbound calls and you need to acquire further time credits, your questioning is so important, especially those first few questions.

Good questioning is key when fact finding and building rapport. Remember to use your open and closed questions correctly and ensure that the questions you ask and more importantly the answers you receive move the call forwards whilst at the same time building rapport.

And yes, once again…good research is so important! You'll have much more to speak about, you'll build much more rapport and you'll find the research is what acquired you the time credits you required.

Now, unless you know you're calling the prospect directly you'll more than likely need to speak to someone within the business who'll either pass you through to them or will pass on their direct number, as you know I like to call this person the head of first impressions.

In previous chapters I discussed using positive language, that's why I don't like the word 'gatekeeper' as it already paints a negative picture of someone who is there to protect the prospect and not let you pass through. This is rarely the case, just because a company employs a receptionist to answer the phone for them doesn't mean the influencers and decisions makers don't want to speak to you and doesn't mean the head of first impressions is in defensive mode, that's what some automatically assume, or will tell you because that's been their experience. That doesn't mean this will be your reality!

Just because other salespeople might inadvertently be telling the head of first impressions that they are expecting not to get through to the prospect, and then don't get through isn't necessarily going to be your experience, it's not been mine.

Some salespeople decide not to turn their charm button on until they speak to a prospect, so the poor head of first impressions has to listen to someone who makes no effort at all. It's clear in their tone and approach that they've never called before, never spoken to the prospect before and are resigned to receiving a negative response or excuse.

The head of first impressions has rarely been told not to transfer sales calls, but often decides themselves whether to transfer a call based on many factors. The most important factor is YOU, if they want to transfer you they will, that's why you need the head of first impressions to like you.

Don't pitch the head of first impressions! because they aren't there to be sold to.

They know themselves they are there to promote their company in a positive light, by answering telephone calls with professionalism and efficiency, they know better than anyone that they are often the first impression you have of their business.

They are aware that they will receive calls from new and existing customers, friends and family of employees and from other businesses with mutual interests, that include sales calls.

Many of them will work alongside salespeople so know and often appreciate the hard work that goes into acquiring new business. They will have transferred many calls from new prospects to their own internal sales team. Can you imagine how many times one of their sales team has said they are expecting a call from a prospect and to let them know when they're on the line, especially if they are on another call. The head of first impressions will now know and appreciate that the call is important.

Remember, you're only doing what those same salespeople are doing in their own business, you're lead generating, prospecting and shouting from the rooftops about how great your products and/or or services are.

Your investment in the head of first impressions is in terms of asking them if they're having a good day at the start of the call, interacting with them on a personal level throughout the call and ensuring you ask for their name at the end of the call. If you were answering the phone all day and none of the calls were for you, wouldn't you want people to make a little more effort to be nice to you.

If you don't speak to your prospect on the first attempt, then on your next call you can speak to the head of first impressions by name, it makes a huge difference. It can often take a few attempts to speak to your prospects, so each call is valuable in terms of what you speak to the head of first impressions about and more importantly how you record this information. Ask them on a Monday if they've had a nice weekend, or, on a Friday if they've got any plans. You'll start to record information about the head of first impressions that will help you build rapport with them when you call back.

As an example, if the head of first impressions mentions they are having a weekend away, ensure you ask about this when you call back, these things build rapport and give you a much better chance of getting through to the prospect or acquiring valuable information such as the prospects movements, direct dial numbers, email addresses etc.

The head of first impressions can also share with you valuable information such as current supplier names etc. It's asking the right questions in a soft and non-invasive way. Each time you speak to the head of first impressions might include one small "oh by the way, do you know…" type question at the end of a call. You'll soon have a dossier of information.

Also, bear in mind that the prospect you're wanting to speak to might not even be the right person! The head of first impressions can let you know if you're contact is the right person and if not provide the correct name.

Top tip:

If there are more than one head of first impressions, you can use this to your advantage. Let's say you've been speaking to Rachel and when you call and say, "Hi Rachel" you hear "no, it's Karen", you can then inflate your relationship to Rachel and your prospect. You might find this is enough to be put through to the boss, or to acquire more valuable info. Now is also the time to build rapport with Karen too, especially if you'll be calling back soon.

Now, I've covered research already within this book and I've stressed its importance. With good research and strategy, you'll improve not only your chances of speaking to the prospect but also having plenty to say, share and discuss when you get hold of them. You'll build rapport and gain trust & confidence.

Note taking is a skill in itself and an important part of your telesales and telemarketing role. Each and every time you call your prospect, is another opportunity to acquire knowledge, and knowledge is power. Whether you speak to the prospect or not, you'll still often acquire important information. Whatever information you acquire, consider how you can best utilise it to gain an advantage.

You might use a CRM, if so, update it often and ensure the information is correct. The best notes for yourself are often the ones that express a flavour of the call, something that might seem irrelevant to others, but you know it sparks an interest in your prospect.

Also, prospects like familiarity, let me explain. Not all prospects will remember you or remember much of the last call you had with them. It'll obviously depend on the time gap between calls and how rememberable you were. So, if the prospect uses a certain word, certain phrase or expresses a certain view, record this information within your notes. Why? Well, it'll ensure the prospect knows that you must have previously spoken to them because that's exactly what they say / would have said.

So, what's the difference between Telesales and Telemarketing?

They are essentially the same thing in terms of outbound calling prospects; however, you'll often find that Telesales people will have the ability to sell their products & services in terms of closing their own deals. Whereas Telemarketing people will often source new leads and book appointments for others. It does not always mean this of course, in the end it's just a job title.

Most salespeople have a job title such as Sales Executive, Sales Advisor, Sales Manager etc, or a title that doesn't even have sales within it, such as Business Development Manager or Account

Manager. If your role is doing any of what I've mentioned a moment ago, spending all of your time on the phone then you'll likely be working in either Telesales or Telemarketing.

In both roles, you're doing plenty of selling, you're selling yourself, your business and of course you'll always be selling your products & services even if someone else actually closes the deals.

b) FIELD SALES

Field sales often means 'life on the road'.

You'll be out and about meeting prospects & customers often at their offices.

You'll either have appointments booked for you or you'll book your own, or a mix of both.

If you really are wanting to progress in sales and do great things, I'd always suggest that you have the ability to book your own appointments. The amount of appointments you book will obviously depend on whether you have someone sourcing leads and booking appointments for you, or, whether you have enough leads to hit your targets, earn the commission you want & expect, and achieve your goals.

Even if you have a Telemarketing team booking appointments for you, you can still assist them with at least sourcing a few new leads and opportunities for them. You are their eyes and ears out and about, so at least hand them opportunities to pursue with a view to booking you more appointments. It's win-win.

Let me explain a typical scenario with a prospect who is also the decision maker, this will give you a flavour for the role and also some handy tips.

You're in a reception area and your prospect comes to greet you.

You shake hands and the prospect takes you to their office or a meeting room.

You need to walk and talk, ideally before you sit down. This is often just informal chit chat, but that's fine. Engage in conversation and keep it flowing after you've sat down. The conversation needs to have nothing to do with why you're attending the meeting. The point is you want to build a rapport with the prospect before you start getting 'down to business'.

Now, of course you'll be guided by the prospect, if you're being encouraged to get on with it or the prospect isn't the chatty type that's fine but if you've done your research and you're also an opportunist you'll find things to talk about that the prospect will engage with. That's why research is so important, as you read in **Chapter 7. RESEARCH AND STRATEGY**.

As I mentioned in **Chapter 2. SALES FUNDAMENTALS** section **41. WHEN YOU OPEN AND CLOSE THE BOOK IN A MEETING**, I always think it's a good idea to place on the desk your PC, book, folder etc but DO NOT open your books or switch on your PC. Have them pushed to one side a little to indicate that you're obviously here to talk business but this is your personal chat time and you're getting to know one another. Many prospects will appreciate the fact your easing into the meeting and taking time to get to know them.

The prospect will be judging you from the get-go, if before you've even opened your book they're thinking 'seems a nice person' you're off to a great start. If you don't place anything on the desk, the prospect might feel a little more obliged to push you along a bit as it'll look like you think you've got all day. The prospect seeing your items on the desk, indicates things to come, so they'll relax a little more into the friendly chat you're having.

At the point you OPEN your book (folder, PC etc) is the point where you're now talking business, try to delay this for as long as you can and as long as the prospect is happy to chat.

218

If you're offered a drink at the start of the meeting accept one, even if you don't drink hot drinks, learn to like them! It buys you more chat time and you'll often find the prospect will join you too. The meeting takes on a different tone when you're having a coffee together or supping a brew. A good rule of thumb is to wait until the drink arrives and see if you can get halfway through it before you've even talked business.

If during the meeting you're offered a second drink, ask the prospect if they'll join you. If they say they're not having a drink then you say "No, I'm fine too". If they say yes, then say "Yes, I'd love one". A second drink can sometimes simply mean your prospect is thirsty although it's often a sign the prospect is happy for the meeting to continue and can see that the meeting still has plenty of life and time left in it.

Back to the start of the meeting and before you've opened your book, you'll get better at this with each meeting. What you don't want to do, is to chat for too long and outstay your welcome before you've even talked about your products & services or your quote if you're already at this stage. You don't want to run out of time either.

If you're in a meeting where you're actually quoting the prospect and you've got a deal in principle, you must start with an overview of the DIP agreed then lead onto how you've achieved the DIP. If you haven't got a DIP in place, then you need to try and establish one before you open the book.

It's as simple as asking before you've opened the book, if you achieve this, that and the other what's the likelihood of you walking away with a deal today? You choose the 'this, that and other' (based on what you know, or what they tell you).

The worst thing for you to do, is to attend a meeting, refuse a drink, engage in little or no small talk and then open your book and get down to talking business, assuming that the prospect won't be making a decision today. You'll be done in no time; you'll have built no rapport and you might just have blown your chances of closing a deal.

People buy from people! So be yourself, be liked and build rapport.

Now, closing the book is as important as opening the book. When you CLOSE the book, you are indicating to the prospect that your meeting is coming to an end.

If you're quoting the prospect and you're wanting a decision, then by closing the book before you've asked for a decision is always the wrong move.

The book staying open is your way of saying that 'I'm still quoting', 'still negotiating' and 'still wanting a decision within this meeting'.

A closed book is a sign that you're not offering further negotiation and might be seen as you are leaving the decision with the prospect to be made at another time, whereas you want the decision now.

If you're not able to get a decision within the meeting or you're not at the quoting stage yet, then your conversation with the prospect after closing the book is vitally important. By closing the book you've signalled that you're no longer talking business and the meeting is coming to an end. This is the best time to get your DIP if you've not quoted yet. It won't seem important to the prospect at that time in terms of what they'll agree to in principle, but you will sure remind them at the start of the next meeting.

Closing the book is also another opportunity to have a few minutes of personal chat. As with when you set up, leave your items on the desk and pushed to one side, books closed, and PC switched off. If you pack all your items away in your bag or briefcase, you'll encourage the prospect to stand up and walk you out to reception. Again, this is about timing and not outstaying your welcome. You'll get better at reading the signs the more you do it. I always enjoy being out and about and

220

meeting prospects & customers. My car and phone are essentially my office for most of the time.

However, there is great value in the time you spend in your office (be that at work or home office), especially if you're quoting the prospects yourself. Get into the routine of ensuring that you follow up your meetings with a message (at the end of each day) to your prospects to thank them for their time and to reiterate what your next move is in terms of quoting & timescales.

Top tip: Also ensure you ask a question, it doesn't matter what the question is, as long as it encourages a response. The reason for this, is you need a reply, as it'll mean you know the message has been received and understood.

If your meetings are booked for you and it's not already standard practice for you to contact the prospect prior to meeting them, then get in touch with them as any interaction you can have with them is great. Ideally, if you can send them an invite on LinkedIn and they accept then great as they can see your profile, background etc

If you're given a business card by your prospects and it includes a mobile number, then great only use this from now on when you call them. Direct contact is ideal.

Of course, the type of contact you have will depend on your relationship with them. If you're meeting went well and you're building rapport then you can text them too, as the response you'll receive is often much quicker.

If you're not given a business card, or it doesn't include a mobile number, ask them if they have a company mobile and if so, could you have their number. Alternatively, ask if they have a direct dial number. What you're trying to avoid is a situation where you call the prospect on the main company telephone number and you have to jump through hoops to get them back on the phone.

If you've already got to know the head of first impressions, and they work from a reception area, thank them on your way in or out of the meeting. Or, call them afterwards to say thanks. Remember, you might not have closed your deal yet, so you still need their help and you need them to know that you're at this advanced stage.

If you haven't got to know the head of first impressions, as you didn't book the appointment then still try and make yourself known to them. I've been in meetings where I've took a packet of biscuits to share with my prospects and then on the way out, I've left the rest of the packet with the head of first impressions or someone else in the office. It's a small gesture but one that always attracts nice attention.

I'd have customers for over 10 years and find that the team still expected cakes or biscuits whenever I turned up for a meeting. That first meeting when the customer was a prospect, set the future tone, I love it!

In field sales you need to be presentable and dress smart.

You need to be punctual!

You need to have good conversational skills.

You need to be organised.

You need to be able to forecast, it's so important for you and your management team.

You need to appreciate that you'll often be up early and late home, especially if your appointments are early or late and you've got a long distance to travel to and from them.

Most of all though, you need to able to close deals!

c) ACCOUNT MANAGEMENT

Often, account management involves managing a base of existing customers with a view to not only retaining the customer in terms of renewal, but also selling additional products & services to them.

Account managers also provide support that customers require, often within a contract period.

The role of an account manager is an important one. They are often the conduit between the customer and the business. They will often support their own internal customer service and support teams too.

Some account managers work exclusively with existing customers that they've either inherited when they took their role or have acquired themselves.

Some account managers have the ability (or are targeted) to acquire new business themselves and convert prospects into new customers.

Some account managers only work on new business and don't have the ability to interact with or renew existing customers.

Like with all roles, for some they will do a mix of all if this.

If you work exclusively with your existing customers, then consider working closer with your new business sales team as there are so many new opportunities that can be acquired via recommendations, referred business etc.

I'd be surprised if/why your existing salespeople aren't already asking you for help in this area, even more surprised if/why your business doesn't encourage and support this throughout your company.

In summary, the point of this (brief) chapter was to inform you that there are so many different types of sales roles, plenty more than what I've already mentioned and each with a different flavour.

In the end, it's about finding a sales role that allows you to flourish and allows your natural sales skills to shine. A sales role that fulfils your goals and provides the ability for you to earn the money you want, expect and need.

There is often a big difference in the pay gaps and additional benefits between these sales roles, this will depend on the size of employer and the value of the products & services they sell.

The best advice I can give you is this, find an employer and a product and/or service that can fulfil your goals at that time.

Remember, your goals are like stepping stones, so if you're new to sales find a role that lets you spread your wings and try new things. Your sales career will change and move in line with your goals and more importantly your ability to close deals. The more successful you are at closing deals, the more you'll earn and the hungrier and driven you'll become.

If you're selling a mass appeal product that pays little commission, then you'll obviously need to sell in large quantities.

If you're selling a niche product, that pays great commission then you'll need to target your prospects carefully and work strategically.

It's about finding the right fit for you and the most suitable environment for your personality, sales ability and potential to fulfil your goals.

In an ideal world, you'll be selling something you are excited about and care about, and you'll be selling a product and/or service that customers want! You'll be working for an employer that pays a great basic wage, achievable targets and a great commission too. You'll be working for an employer that values YOU! …Its most important commodity.

If your world is not presenting as 'ideal' then you might decide to set up your own business. A great business can be created on the back of a great idea, a gap in the market or simply the desire to succeed on your own terms.

I will be writing more books, in this series of books. Some of the books will include subjects specifically on these very subjects, particularly sales, and also entrepreneurship.

Chapter 9. EMOTIONS:
Your mind and your heart

Getting your head and your heart singing in tune is so important.

What do I mean by this?

We've all heard a phrase like, "My heart says one thing but my heads says another". What this means is that the rationale, sensible and logical side of us often use our head, our mind, essentially our brain to determine an outcome.

Whereas our hearts are often the things we want the most, it can sometimes be hopeful and not always based on sense or logic.

I appreciate that most people will tell you that statistically you're not going to win the lottery, so your head will use logic to determine this makes sense and you'll accept it, but your heart still tells you to buy a ticket, because…what if?

Listen, someone will win, and I guarantee that those winners will have also used their heads to tell them they probably wouldn't.

Where's our gut in all of this? We've all said, "I have a gut feeling about this". Has this come from your head or your heart? you'll find it's often a bit of both.

Is it your head or heart that tells you if you should be afraid? if you should be excited? if you should be grateful? Or, if you can or can't do something?

You are in control of your emotions, and you can use them effectively as and when required. They are your personal internal resources and you can utilise and benefit from them whenever you want.

Life will have its ups and downs and a few bumps in the road should be expected and anticipated along the way. It's your head and your heart that will support you, guide you and reward you if you choose to control them. You are the boss of your internal settings, you control everything.

Let me digress for a short moment:

I love lyrics to songs, especially lyrics that can motivate or inspire me.

As I've already mentioned in this book, a great example of a song that can motivate is 'One Moment in Time' by Whitney Houston. The writers, Albert Hammond and John Bettis wrote this song for the 1988 Olympics. Please let me persuade you to listen to this song whilst also reading the lyrics, it's very powerful.

There is a line in the song that says, "To taste the sweet I face the pain", a beautiful line.

For me, (relevant to what I've just said regarding the ups and downs along the way) this line is so true in sales and in life. If you work hard, practice and dig deep emotionally, when tough times present themselves (and they will) you'll be ready, you've anticipated it and you'll be in a much better position to overcome your challenges when they present themselves.

There are sources of inspiration all around us that can pull at our heart strings, engage our minds and fan the flames of desire within our hearts. My thoughts and my feelings are a huge reason why I've been successful in sales and in life. I have a strong mind and a big heart.

I'm positive, confident, focussed, driven, caring, compassionate and most of all honest with myself and others.

I realised as a teenager that negative thoughts can only hurt me. Since then, I choose to fill my mind with positive, happy thoughts. Rather than doubt myself and say, 'can I?' I choose to say, 'I can, and I will'.

Of course, I have ups and downs, hit bumps in the road and from time to time life just gets in the way. It's during these times I also have to dig deep, refocus and pick myself back up. I don't indulge in negative emotions; I fight them and choose to overcome them. I was expecting and anticipating a bump in road so was prepared, ready and able to use my head and heart to pick me back up, dust myself down and send me back on my way. I knew that to taste the sweet I would need to face the pain.

I have over 20 years of experience managing people, and I've often found that talking about emotions isn't easy for most. It's a trust thing, most people aren't confident sharing their inner most thoughts and feelings. This is often because most people have never really been honest with themselves let alone others.

The journey I've been on with so many people has been built on trust. We work at your pace, in your time and on your terms.

I'm no expert on this subject, and of course there are some wonderful professionals that can assist you with your emotional health & well-being. I've encouraged, supported and also paid for others to seek professional help. My role is to care, acknowledge and support others who need help with their emotional health.

I have so much respect for people that ask for help, it all starts with you. If you know you're struggling and know you're suffering then please understand you don't need to know why, before you ask for help. You might have no idea why you're feeling like you do, or you might think you know why and can't do anything to change this.

The tips and techniques I write about in this chapter will help you with your emotional health & well-being, will give you a stronger mind and will encourage you to better control your thoughts and feelings. However, if you know you need help on a much deeper emotional level than this, please seek professional help.

You purchased this book because you are looking for some help, guidance & support in sales. Continue this journey (if required) and seek help, guidance and support with your emotional health and well-being.

Look, now is the time to open up, ask yourself the important questions and answer them honestly. If moving forward, you're then able to share your feelings with others, even better.

In **Chapter 2. SALES FUNDAMENTALS**, you read about the importance of how you start and end each day. You also read how important it was to react and adapt throughout the day.

How you start your day is essential to best determine what your day will look like, 'Win the morning and you'll win the day!'

Has anyone ever asked you if you'd got out the wrong side of the bed? Of course, they are asking you this because they feel you're grumpy, negative, sad etc. Whatever side of the bed you get out of ensure it's with a positive attitude and with a spring in your step.

Get yourself into a routine, one which allows you time to prepare yourself physically and mentally for the day ahead. Ensure you have the time to eat a healthy breakfast and to gather your thoughts rather than rushing out the door creating chaos around you.

You must understand and appreciate that your thoughts are controlled by you, your mood is determined by you, your hopes, dreams, wants and expectations for the day ahead are all yours to create, decide and fulfil.

Daily life will challenge your head and heart constantly, it will try and give and take throughout the day.

Daily life will also give you plenty of opportunities to smile, laugh, feel empowered, feel grateful and feel successful.

You must open your eyes, mind & heart and take advantage of these important moments throughout each day. Open your senses, and you'll begin to notice sounds, smells and positive vibrations like never before. You'll soon realise that you yourself are creating and shaping daily life because of your wants and needs for these moments to happen. It's the law of attraction working at its best.

However, daily life will also try and affect your mood, shake your confidence and test your resolve. Don't worry, life hasn't got a hidden agenda against you, the universe wants you to do well. These blips, hurdles or bumps in the road are life's way of keeping you in check, keeping you focused and keeping you on point. If your head and your heart are singing as one, if your eyes are keenly and firmly on the prize and if you are expecting the unexpected, you'll win and keep winning because you'll adapt, adjust, pick yourself up when required and keep moving forward.

Your senses are so important to stimulating the way you want your head and heart to feel. They are like battery chargers for your soul.

Let's look at visual and audio stimuli.

VISUAL:

Place pictures around your working environment that give you the visual stimulation you require to succeed. Split these pictures into 5 groups.

Love

The first group is love.

These can include family photos, your child's drawing, your pet dog etc. When things are going well these photos will speak to you and tell you 'well done' and that they're 'proud of you'. When things are not going well, they'll pick you up and tell you 'it's ok', 'you can do it', 'don't give up' and guess what? they're still 'proud of you'.

Inspiration

The second group is inspiration.

Sure, the love pictures will inspire, but this group is for the inspirations in your life outside of your family and friends. These people might include sporting hero's, music icons, movie stars, entrepreneurs, gurus, leaders, teachers, charity workers etc.

There might be inspiring people involved in inspiring stories that pulls on your heart strings. If so, channel the energy of these people and these stories. These are the people and or/stories that mean something to you, they've touched you, inspired you and are part of your life.

Wants & expectations

The 3rd group is wants and expectations.

Your wants can be anything, and it's fine if they are material things too!

If you want a new car, a new house, a holiday or a new watch, then place these pictures on the wall.

If you want a million pounds, then write a cheque to yourself with a future date on it.

If you want a promotion or your own business, then print a business card with your job title and/or company name on it.

Remember, thoughts become things. *(Q) What do you want?*

Your happy place

The 4th group is your happy place.

Sure, for many their happy place will be home, and that's fine.

However, for this, dig a little deeper and think of the one place on this beautiful earth, or in your beautiful mind where you feel truly happy, blessed and at peace with yourself. It's this happy place that you will take yourself too often (in your mind) when you require it. It's a place of safety and a place you can go to anytime you like, it'll drown out the noise around you and provide you a reset and recharge button whenever required. This happy place might be a moment in time, with an imprinted happy memory you have, if so, that's fine too.

I did!

The 5th group is something that represents 'I did!'

If you hit your target, acquire your largest order or win an award etc, then take an image of something that represents and recognises this such as a photo of the sales whiteboard, a payslip, a sales report, an email from your boss, the award itself, a press release etc.

You need to remind yourself that 'I did' and tell yourself you will again. This visual representation of 'I did' is not to be used as a way to take your foot off the gas, or to live off this one success forever. It's there to inspire you to do it again, repeat it and beat it. It's there to remind you of what you did, how you did it and how you felt before, during and after it. If you did it, then do it again…and often.

AUDIO

Music specifically, is a wonderful resource to affect your mood.

A specific song or piece of music can resonate a memory that can take you back to a moment in time, or can provide a shared memory of family, friends or an eventful moment in your life.

In the same way that taste and smell can evoke powerful memories so can sound, especially music.

For me, it's the lyrics within songs that evokes powerful emotions within me. Great lyrics accompanied by great music can be very inspiring.

I often listen to a classical piece of music written by the great Mozart, it's Clarinet Concerto in A Major. At 37 seconds into the concerto, is when my wife entered the room and walked down the aisle to marry me. For me, this evokes such powerful emotions, I love the way it makes me feel. Beautiful music for a beautiful lady.

The point here is to use whatever works for you.

I always wonder why some people choose to listen to the news before work, it's never good news. Sure, you might want to quickly scan the headlines and keep abreast of what's going on in the world as sure it might crop up in conversation, but why would you want to start your day like this.

You need to find your happy place and focus on the day ahead and reiterate why you're doing this. This can't be done 1 minute before the phones start ringing, your head and heart need at least half hour of preparation before your workday begins, to get into the zone.

Is there a taste and/or smell that evokes powerful memories for you? For me, the taste of apple pie always evokes wonderful memories of my nan, wow her pastry was the best! Of course, I think of my nan and grandad often, but they are passing thoughts that pass over me like the breeze. When I evoke memories like nan's apple pie, it further evokes a string of memories about my nan and grandad some of which I haven't thought about for many years. I love how happy and content it makes me feel, of course there is a little bit of sadness thrown in too, but that's because I miss them.

The smell of sea air evokes memories of holidays with my family. The smell never changes, that salty, sandy, seaweed smell takes me instantly back to when I was 6 or 7 and in my wellies on the beach looking for crabs and treasure! I loved being a kid, such happy times.

If your eyes, mouth, ears and nose can evoke such powerful memories, then you should learn to use these senses to your advantage. You can choose what to look at, what to listen to, what to eat and what to smell whenever you want, choose and need to.

So, wake up and look at your favourite photo, the one that makes you feel like getting up on the right side of the bed and racing with destiny. Listen to music before work, it might be a specific song that evokes a memory, or it might simply be a specific genre of music that gets you in the mood. Prepare something nice for lunch, where you know your 'yummy' tones, will be followed by a happy thought or memory.

You get the gist, you know what works for you, so encourage these emotions and use them to help you succeed in sales and in life. As I said in previous chapters, your emotional health and well-being are so important, not just when working in sales but more importantly to life.

Getting your mind and your heart in the zone is essential when it comes to the practical side of sales, the 'doing'.

I'm sure if you were to ask the hundreds of people I've coached and mentored over the last 2 decades, many would say they benefited from a new appreciation and understanding of their emotional health & well-being.

If you're happy, be happy! Your prospects & customers will often join you in your happy place and often reward you for it.

If you're not happy, then you need to find that happy place in your mind and your heart. If this is easier said than done, then you need to address your emotional health & well-being and help yourself to take the steps necessary towards happiness.

Please allow me to repeat what I said in **Chapter 2. SALES FUNDAMENTALS** section **68. BE HAPPY**. It's obvious I know, but if you're not happy you'll struggle to succeed. Happiness is a very personal emotion; one person's definition of happiness is different to another. Understand what makes YOU happy and work towards this. If you're not happy your prospects & customers will know, maybe even before you do. You might think you can fake it, but you can't.

You might be unhappy with certain things in your life, but with a clear direction, with positivity, confidence and all the other key ingredients you've read within this book, you know you'll get to a happier place, if you're not already there.

If you're unhappy, it's important to address 'why' and take the appropriate action to change how you're feeling. This involves being honest and open with yourself and sharing your thoughts and feelings with others. You can't fake happiness, and why would you want to?

Wanting to be happy and taking action towards your future happiness is a relief in itself, you've taken control of your emotional health & well-being and you'll instantly feel a little better.

So be happy NOW in this moment, especially whilst doing sales, your prospects & customers don't need to know anything other than you're happy now, today.

Could you be happier, maybe? But the point is you're not unhappy and you're working towards a happier place.

When you smile and dial it makes such a positive difference to your success in sales and also how you feel emotionally about your daily role. Your prospects & customers will appreciate this, you'll build better rapport and you'll be liked so much more.

In summary, the emotional side of sales is so important. Your heart and your mind are important things to understand, they have personal settings that need programming and constant nurturing.

I'll dedicate a future book about emotional health & wellbeing, it's so important and I care deeply about this subject.

Chapter 10. WHAT NOW?

It's chapter 10, we've made it to this final chapter together on this journey of learning and discovery. What you do NOW, TODAY and for the rest of your time in sales is so important.

So, what now? let's recap a little

We started this book with **Chapter 1.WHY SALES?**

You asked yourself why sales? and I'm sure your answers were (and are) clear, positive, focused and driven for success. You said, "I can, and I will", and you want and expect to be successful.

Your 'why' is what gets you up in the morning, your 'why' is what gets you on the phone or in-front of prospects, your 'why' is what picks you up when you're down or keeps your feet on the ground when things are going well.

Your 'why' is why you look for self-improvement and why you aren't afraid of critique.

In the end, your 'why' is the reason WHY you'll achieve your goals and fulfil your potential.... why? it's because you had a why! Good for you.

We moved onto **Chapter 2. SALES FUNDAMENTALS: Principles, Key Ingredients and Tips & Techniques for successful selling**

As you know, all successful salespeople have built their careers on solid sales foundations, that's certainly the case for me. I'm confident it will now be the same for you too!

You now appreciate that these solid sales foundations are built over time and are acquired 'on the job'. Sure, you'll acquire knowledge from books, videos and training courses. However, you know that experience, understanding and appreciation can only be gained by 'doing' sales yourself, which is what you will do to the best of your ability.

You also appreciate that all successful salespeople will agree that understanding, embracing and adopting a core set of sales fundamentals is the key to a successful sales career and is the strength that supports those all-important solid sales foundations. You're now ready to embrace and adopt these sales fundamentals as you've acquired a better understanding of them.

If your 'what now?' is all about taking action, taking control and shaping your own destiny! You'll fulfil your true potential.

In **Chapter 3. WORDS, TIMING & TONE: What you say, when you say, how you say** focused on your sales pitch. As you now know…what you say, when you say and how you say are the key ingredients to a successful sales pitch. Remember, you'll close many more deals on the back of a well-constructed, well thought out and well delivered sales pitch.

In **Chapter 4. CLOSING: If you're not closing then you aren't selling**, we looked at a few closing techniques such as a 'deal in principle' (DIP), and I'm sure you'll take these (& many more) into your daily sales role.

You now appreciate that 'the close' starts at the very beginning of the customer journey and builds throughout your sales pitch and isn't something that magically appears at the end of your sales pitch by surprise. You know that if you're struggling to close deals, you'll find its all the things you've done or more importantly 'not done' beforehand that's the real issue.

Always remember, a close is made on every sale, either you sell to the prospect and/or customer or they close the door on you.

Moving onto **Chapter 5. OBJECTION HANDLING: Use their excuses to your advantage**, we looked at how you can better prepare for the objections and excuses you'll receive from your prospects & customers.

I've now equipped you with the tools required to overcome objections & excuses and to use them to your advantage.

After reading **Chapter 6. INFLUENCER OR DECISION MAKER** you're now better equipped to 'influence the influencer' and to get yourself in front of more decision makers. You'll use the tips & techniques provided to generate more leads, acquire more customers and close more deals.

A common theme throughout the book has been Research. In **Chapter 7. RESEARCH AND STRATEGY: Knowledge with a plan of action.** I reiterated that research is essential! and I'm sure it will now be a key part of your lead generation strategy and a key tool you'll utilise in gaining more sales.

If you adopt the advice I've given you, I'm sure you'll get one step ahead of the competition and more importantly one step closer to your prospects before you've even spoken to them. You'll see instant results from the research you'll do.

You'll soon see that good research will also enable you to have a better strategy in terms of how you'll engage your prospects & customers and how they'll engage with you.

In **Chapter 8. SALES ROLES: Telesales & Telemarketing, Field Sales and Account Management** we looked at the various sales roles.

I encouraged you to try different sales roles throughout your sales career as it will determine what you're best at, what you most enjoy and where you're able to maximise your true potential both professionally and financially. To reiterate, it's about finding the right fit for you and the most suitable environment for your personality, sales ability and potential to fulfil your goals.

In an ideal world, you'll be selling something you are excited about and care about, and you'll be selling a product and/or service that customers want! You'll be working for an employer that pays a great basic wage, achievable targets and a great commission too. You'll be working for an employer that values YOU! ...Its most important commodity.

Add to this your ability to adopt the sales fundamentals you've learned within this book and you'll be an all-round Sales Whizz®.

In **Chapter 9. EMOTIONS: Your mind and your heart** we focussed on your emotional health & wellbeing. You might recall, I said this was the most important chapter I'd written in this book! It really was and is.

This chapter was only the start (I hope) for you to discuss, understand and nurture your emotional health.

Your thoughts and feelings led you to buy this book and to read it, and it's these same emotions that will determine what you do next.

I asked you to dig a little deeper emotionally in this chapter, did you? If so, good for you. I want you to continue to acquire a much deeper understanding of yourself. If you can tap into the wonderful resources which are your mind and your heart, you'll not only give yourself the best chance to succeed in sales but also learn to discover, understand and appreciate 'your' happiness.

So, WHAT NOW?

It's so important for you to continue to embrace and adopt the advice I've provided in this book and even more important to continue your journey for self-improvement.

This book isn't a 'get rich quick' book or a blueprint for automatic success overnight. This book is simply taking things back to basics and allowing you to reset and move forwards.

I want you to be stubborn about your goals and flexible about your methods.

Why don't you consider finding a colleague, friend or family member who is also working in sales, or wanting to work in sales and ask them to also purchase this book? You might find that it encourages you to converse with them, share your thoughts, feelings & opinions and keeps you focussed on the journey ahead.

Or, you might prefer to go this one alone for now and let your results be the thing that gets people talking? It's your call (… although from a sales perspective I'd much rather you helped promote my book!), see I'm always selling too, …it's what we do.

Also, our journey doesn't have to end here, it's only just begun. I'd like you to send me a personal message. I'd love to know how I've helped you, as it will continue to quench my thirst for helping others.

Please send me an invite on LinkedIn and let me know you've read my book. Once connected, you can then message me with some valuable feedback. I also post regular content that you might find useful.

You can also email me via dean@saleswhizz.com

This book was published in 2020 so depending on when you're reading these words, my future books might now already be a reality!

244

Please look out for the others books I've written, and thanks in advance if you purchase them.

All the best, I wish you a happy and successful future.

Now at the top of your voice say these all-important words, they really are a self-fulfilling prophecy … **"I CAN, AND I WILL".**

End.

Printed in Poland
by Amazon Fulfillment
Poland Sp. z o.o., Wrocław

59852597R00139